REFERENCE READINESS

REFERENCE READINESS

A Manual for Librarians, Researchers, and Students

Fourth Edition, Revised and Updated

AGNES ANN HEDE

LIBRARY PROFESSIONAL PUBLICATIONS
1990

Library of Congress Cataloging-in-Publication Data

Hede, Agnes Ann.
Reference readiness : a manual for librarians,
researchers, and students / Agnes Ann Hede.
4th ed., rev. and updated.
p.   cm.
1. Reference books—Bibliography.
2. Reference services (Libraries)   I. Title.
Z1035.1.H4   1990
011'.02—dc20   90-30394
ISBN 0-208-02228-7 (alk. paper).
ISBN 0-208-02229-5 (pbk.: alk. paper).

The paper used in this publication meets the minimum requirements
of American National Standard for Information Sciences—Permanence
of Paper for Printed Library Materials, ANSI Z39.48-1984.

This Fourth Edition is
for my incomparable mother
Balbina Ann Musial Hede
and to
Lewis W. Guiss, M.D., in gratitude

CONTENTS

PREFACE

The concept and format of *Reference Readiness* were developed by Sylvia Ziskind, who wrote the first edition and was my coauthor for the second edition. Her enthusiasm for the field and her appreciation and knowledge of books have influenced her students, colleagues, and friends, and provided a vital example of the true substance of librarianship.

The approach to *Reference Readiness* remains as she expressed it in the introduction to the first edition: "A reference librarian is, in a sense, a magician, and in this book I have tried to capture the art and mystery of bringing to view that which a moment before was unperceived. I have always experienced the joy of contest in my work as a librarian and I hope to impart that spirit to others who choose to work with reference materials."

ACKNOWLEDGMENTS

I thank the editors and publishers who so generously commented on the coverage of their publications that appeared in the third edition, and who provided review copies of their new editions and titles. Their interest was of inestimable help.

Acknowledgment is given to Dr. Rosemarie Riechel for her assistance with the chapter "Computer Sources and Services."

The consideration and support of my editor, Virginia H. Mathews, and of the Granada Hills Library regional and branch managers, Nina Wilson and Christina H. Bzyl, are gratefully acknowledged. With special appreciation for her agreeing to go the second time around, I thank Susan Barnhart for her skillful typing and thoughtful assistance in the preparation of the manuscript.

INTRODUCTION

Reference Readiness is intended for the student librarian, the practicing librarian, and the researcher who wish to learn or to review the range of general, basic reference sources in the English language. It is not intended as a text for reading *about* reference books, but rather to be used in conjunction with the examination of the works described to learn what they contain, and when and how to use them. The chief purpose of the book is to provide the student or beginning librarian with the confidence that appropriate sources can be selected to answer diverse questions.

To accomplish this purpose, selected titles are presented, with guides to their formats and contents, and with examples to demonstrate the kind of information that can be found in them. Questions are included to reinforce what has been learned and to enable the reader to make the fullest use of the works, or to stimulate additional study and comparative analysis of other works.

There are excellent books available for comprehensive bibliographies of reference sources, and for discussions of reference techniques that might be used together with *Reference Readiness*. For detailed, authoritative and extensive bibliographies with annotations, refer to *Guide to Reference Books* by Eugene P. Sheehy, which is included in the chapter on bibliographies. For concepts, techniques, and trends in reference services, the *Introduction to Reference Work: Reference Services and Reference Processes, v. 2* by William A. Katz (5th ed. N.Y., McGraw-Hill, 1987) is recommended.

For this fourth edition, all entries retained from the previous three were reexamined; titles with new editions, supplements, or title changes were revised and updated. Many new titles were added. Selected out-of-print titles that have been reputably long established and are unique in their content have been included.

Because the printed form of reference sources still provides the foundation for initial study and use, and because those works are continuously being added to microform, online access, and CD-ROM, the entries in *Reference Readiness* describe only the printed sources, except for those works now available only on microform, such as the

National Union Catalog. Reminders that reference sources are abundantly available in various formats are included throughout the book. There is a discussion on computer sources, with a selected bibliography, in chapter 10.

Given the proliferation of general and specialized reference materials, omissions must be expected. This edition, like its predecessors, is neither all-inclusive nor elite in its listings; it is a *selection* of general reference works from which one may advance to others. The large and impressive body of specialized reference sources that exists today is a challenge to the most experienced reference librarian.

The entries within each chapter are in alphabetical order by title, with the exception of those that form a series or interrelated sequence. All of the titles included may be located through the index, which lists authors, editors, and titles.

Because of limited staffing or budget shortages, many librarians in public libraries who did not choose children's services as a specialty must work at the children's reference desk on a regular rotation schedule, or in the absence of the children's librarians. In recognition of this, selected titles of reference books for children are included, but these constitute only an introduction to the basic titles that are available. There are many comprehensive and specialized reference tools for librarians or researchers who are interested in obtaining a broader or in-depth knowledge of the field. You will find some of them cited in the bibliographies of the works described here. It is worth remembering the comment in Virginia Haviland's introduction to her *Children's Literature: A Guide to Reference Sources* (Washington, D.C., Library of Congress, 1966–   ): "Of lists of children's books there is no end."

At the end of each chapter you will find a bibliography of related titles. Many of these additional titles are considered to be as useful and important in their category as those described in the text and should be referred to for a wider knowledge of available reference sources. The chain is unending, for the "additional titles" have bibliographies, companion volumes, and supplements.

As in the previous editions of *Reference Readiness,* those who use libraries and request the assistance of reference librarians are referred to as patrons and readers. Though today "patron" may seem to be a designation that undermines the librarian's professional status, the "comparable worth" of the librarian/information specialist, the term "user," currently accepted by many in the field, has such other negative meanings that it does not seem to be a suitable alternative.

Exception is made for the established terminology of the computer world (as, user-oriented, user-friendly). It is somehow disquieting to think of advising an inquirer that "the librarian is in the stacks with a user," or, with the inquirer present, to tell a colleague that "this user wants. . . ." For a witty, still pertinent discussion as to the choice of these and other terms, read "A Borrower Is a Client Is a Patron Is a User Is a Reader," by Michael Gorman in *American Libraries* (October 1983, p. 597).

Your primary goal in this study should be to learn what the best sources are, what they contain, what makes them unique, and which will provide the most appropriate, complete, authoritative, and efficiently obtained answers to the questions you receive. It is hoped that, with the added confidence that comes with experience, you will begin to enjoy the challenge and accruement of knowledge that reference service brings.

1.

DICTIONARIES

How many people are able to interpret the symbols, abbreviations, and etymologies in a dictionary? How many know whether a dictionary gives the meanings of a word in chronological order, and whether the modern meaning is first or last? How many consult a dictionary only when engaged in word games or crossword puzzles?

In our individual development, after beginning learning with the wonder of seeing, observing, perceiving, and distinguishing, we begin to question. We grow with the joy or anxiety of endlessly asking, "What's this?" "What's that?" "Why?" Then suddenly the free and easy answers are replaced by the instruction that we have to try to find the answer, solve the problem, ourselves. With the direction, "Look it up," we learn that there are various sources to provide the answers, the number, scope, and difficulty of which increase as we grow and learn.

Why, of all the answer sources available—the encyclopedias, handbooks, indexes, bibliographies—does the dictionary seem to present the most intimidating or disliked obstacle? Some adults will admit to not knowing the meaning or pronunciation of a word, to not being able to spell, to wishing their vocabulary could be enlarged, but still they resist the use of a dictionary.

It is hoped that this chapter will remove any negative impressions you may have regarding dictionaries. It is also intended to dispel the idea that "if you've seen one dictionary, you've seen them all!"

Another heading for this chapter might be "Word Books," because that is what it's all about: books that analyze words, trace their history, show how they have been used in the past, and how they are used today. With one exception, this chapter does not include dictionaries limited to specialized areas of knowledge, but is confined to general dictionaries, or word books, with a section on thesaurus titles.

There are many dictionaries designed for children in the elementary and intermediate grades, as well as for high school and college students. You should know about some of the excellent ones and be wary of purchasing any for which you cannot find an authoritative review. It is wise to buy only the best. Examples of these are analyzed in the following pages, and others are cited in the list of additional titles at the end of the chapter. Sources for selection of dictionaries are also described in the chapter on bibliographies.

The demand for foreign-language and bilingual dictionaries in libraries is increasing, as is the number of languages requested. Monolingual dictionaries in a foreign language are compiled according to the same pattern as our English language dictionaries. Words are listed alphabetically, followed by pronunciations, etymologies, and definitions. Quotations are frequently used to clarify a word's meaning with examples of usage. This kind of dictionary requires, of course, that the searcher has a basic familiarity with the language.

The bilingual dictionary provides the meanings of foreign words by giving translations or equivalents in another language. Most bilingual dictionaries have two alphabetical listings (e.g., Italian-English, English-Italian). Such dictionaries are most useful for someone who is learning a new language or needs to translate material written in a foreign language.

People who seek the aid of bilingual dictionaries are many and varied. Librarians should meet the requirements of a widely heterogeneous public by surveying the library's actual and potential clientele to determine the number and kinds of monolingual and bilingual dictionaries that are needed. Fortunately, there are guides for evaluation, annotated bibliographies, and review sources available to help in selection.

It is recommended that you read the introductions to the sections on English-language and foreign-language dictionaries in Eugene P. Sheehy's *Guide to Reference Books* (q.v.), and look through the extensive bibliography of foreign-language dictionaries. Two other comprehensive sources on English-language dictionaries are Marion Sader's *General Reference Books for Adults* and *Reference Books for Young Readers* (q.v.).

<table>
<tr><td>PE
1580
B35</td><td align="right">**THE BARNHART DICTIONARY
OF ETYMOLOGY**
Robert K. Barnhart, Editor;
Sol Steinmetz, Managing Editor
N.Y., H. W. Wilson, 1988. xxvii, 1,284p.</td></tr>
</table>

"The *Barnhart Dictionary of Etymology* records the roots of our language and shows its many points of contact with the other cultures from which it has absorbed new words and new ideas. It is truly an American reference work not only because it pays particular attention to the American aspect of semantic development of English words but also because it bases much of its material on points of view developed by American scholars. This is the first dictionary of etymology to be produced by an editorial staff in collaboration with American scholars from various fields of language study. . . .

"This dictionary is an interpretation of current scholarship. . . . In numberless instances the chronological record has been revised from that of the *Oxford English Dictionary*, drawing the year of first recorded appearance back sometimes as much as two to three hundred years" (Preface).

Following the preface, there are rosters of the editorial and the original committees of contributing scholars, and the editorial staff.

The explanatory notes describe the development of our language, and reiterate the dictionary's special emphasis on American English. There is a listing of the few abbreviations and symbols used, of the language periods cited in the entries, and a pronunciation key. Two essays on the history and development of language precede the main text.

1. As examples of entries, look up *abundant, molecule, Yankee, rhythm, jeans,* and *byte*. Note the dates and sources of first use, and the credit given to other etymological works, as the *OED*. Cross references are shown in small capital letters.

2. At the back of the dictionary, turn to:
   a. A "Glossary of Language Names and Linguistic Terms." Read the clear definitions and some of the interesting descriptions, such as those given for *cognate, Cherokee, Pilipino, Canadian French,* and *back formation*.
   b. A "Glossary of Literary Works Cited in Etymologies." An explanation of the content is at the beginning of each glossary.

Do you find that the aim of the book as expressed in the preface, "to make examples of the development of English an understandable subject for those with no specialized knowledge of language study," was accomplished?

PE
1591
B45

BERNSTEIN'S REVERSE DICTIONARY, 2d ed.
By Theodore M. Bernstein;
revised and expanded by David Grambs
N.Y., Times Books, 1988. xi, 351p.

The editor has retained the introduction to the original edition, written by Theodore M. Bernstein, which explains that "a conventional dictionary lists words alphabetically and gives you their meanings. This unconventional dictionary lists an array of meanings alphabetically and gives you the 'words.' . . . The words it discovers for you are those you have momentarily forgotten or those you never knew or those of whose meanings you were not quite certain" (p. vii). The entire introduction is entertaining and informative, with an anecdote on how the book came into being.

The entries listed in alphabetical order are called the "clue words"—words or phrases that you probably would use to describe the exact word that eludes you. These are immediately followed by the words you might be trying to remember or learn, called the "target words," which are printed in small capitals. The target words are also listed alphabetically in an index at the end of the book.

1. If you are trying to remember, or don't know the term, to describe the use in singing of the syllables *do, re, mi,* etc., you will find an entry under "Musical use vocally of the syllables do, re, mi, etc.," followed by the word, *Solfeggio.* The term is also in the index for target words, with the page number for the clue words.

2. There are five "special or omnibus listings," which appear in boxes in alphabetical sequence by the titles, including Phobias, Manias, Creature Terms, Medical Fields and the nicknames of the states under U.S. State Nicknames.

3. As you stand on a ship facing forward, what is the right side of the ship called? If you know the answer, can you verify it through the use of the target word index?

This *Reverse Dictionary* is a unique and very useful reference aid.

PE
2835
C72

DICTIONARY OF AMERICAN ENGLISH
ON HISTORICAL PRINCIPLES
By Sir William Craigie and James R. Hulbert
Chicago, University of Chicago Press, 1936–44. 4v.

This dictionary was modeled after the *Oxford English Dictionary* (q.v.) and is valuable for its historical focus on American English.

The editors state in the preface that "a historical dictionary of American English must be much more than a collection of Americanisms . . . it must illustrate fully the manifold ways in which the language has been adapted to the country and its inhabitants, and has thus constantly added new shades of meaning to ordinary words, given them a wider currency, or brought them into connection with new conditions and circumstances" (v. 1, p. xi).

The explanation of special lettering and symbols, which appears at the beginning of each volume, is most helpful in developing skill in using the dictionary. The plus sign, for example, "indicates that the word or sense clearly or to all appearances originated within the present limits of the United States" (v. 1, p. xiv).

1. As you glance through any one of the volumes, you will see that the words appearing in boldface type vary in size. The size designates the relative importance of the word either historically or in current usage.

2. Look up any word of your choice. Remember, this work covers the language only through the nineteenth century. Slang and dialectal words are included only if they occurred in the early part of our history, or if they are particularly important. Once you have found your word, try to interpret each symbol. Notice the variety of quotations. *Foolscap* and *foot the bill* are interesting entries.

PE
2835
D5

A DICTIONARY OF AMERICANISMS ON HISTORICAL PRINCIPLES
By Mitford McLeod Mathews
Chicago, University of Chicago Press, 1951. 2v.

The editor clarified his intent by stating in the preface that "as used in the titles of his work, 'Americanism' means a word that originated in the United States. The term includes: outright coinages, as *appendicitis, hydrant, tularemia*; such words as *adobe, campus, gorilla,* which first became English in the United States; and terms such as *faculty, fraternity, refrigerator,* when used in senses first given them in American usage" (p. v).

This is a later work than Craigie's *Dictionary of American English* (q.v.) and is more restrictive in scope.

1. As an illustration of the careful study of the words included, read the section of the preface (p. vii) on the word *alcalde*.

2. An indication of the scholarliness of the work is the care taken in giving sources, dates, and quotations. See the entry *buckshot.* If necessary, refer to the explanation of special lettering and symbols (p. xv), and the list of abbreviations (p. vi) to interpret the information.

   Look in volume 2 under *Molly Maguires.* The explanation given refers to an important period in U.S. labor history.

3. There are words or expressions included that "did not come first or independently into English in the United States" (p. xv). Such words have an asterisk before them, as *homestead.* Notice the historical data and quotations included for this word.

An abridged edition of this work, titled *Americanisms: A Dictionary of Selected Americanisms on Historical Principles,* was issued in 1966 (in print 1988). The entries were selected by Mathews from the original work "in an effort to assure the reader the widest possible range of examples within the limits of this edition" (Preface, p. vii).

If you have not yet seen the two-volume unabridged work, you might enjoy reading some of the varied and unexpected entries, including *gardenia, mockingbird, vaseline,* the *letter E, grass roots,* and *peanut butter*! There are many place names (as *Chisholm Trail*) and American Indian names.

A bibliography of the sources of quotations used is found at the end of the work.

PE
1628
F65

**DICTIONARY OF MODERN ENGLISH
USAGE, 2d ed.
By Henry Watson Fowler,
revised by Sir Ernest Gowers**
Oxford, Clarendon Press, 1965. 725p.

The success and popularity of this work since the publication of the first edition in 1926 is indicated by the fact that it frequently is referred to simply as "Fowler's." The author's blending of scholarship with sharp wit and personal opinions creates a unique dictionary. To gain insight into the personality, idiosyncrasy, and style of Fowler, read the brief preface to the first edition, reprinted in the revised edition, and then read the preface to the revised edition.

Sir Ernest Gowers, the editor of the revised edition, painstakingly preserved Fowler's style. He added a classified guide to simplify the finding of articles.

1. Before searching for a specific topic, turn to any page and read a column or two to enjoy the flavor, or "Fowleresque touch," of this unique volume.

2. You will appreciate the addition of the classified guide as you come to such entries as *swapping horses* and *out of the frying pan*. Note the social awareness and humor reflected in the articles on *false scent* and *meaningless words*.

   As a contrast, see the detailed coverage of the word *between* and the interesting list of eponymous words.

PE 3721 P3	**DICTIONARY OF SLANG AND UNCONVENTIONAL ENGLISH: Colloquialisms and Catch-Phrases, Solecisms and Catechreses, Nicknames and Vulgarisms, 8th ed.**

By Eric Partridge,
edited by Paul Beale
N.Y., Macmillan, 1984. xxix, 1,400p.

In the preface, the editor explains what changes have been made in producing this dictionary from the famous original edition compiled by the late Eric Partridge, who described it as a companion to the *Oxford English Dictionary* (q.v.). The work created much controversy at the time of publication because of its inclusion of vulgarisms, but it has become a standard source.

Begin by reading the arrangement within entries (p. xix), which is followed by an explanation of the dating, a list of bibliographical abbreviations, and abbreviations and signs.

1. It is necessary to understand the abbreviations to interpret the legend given for each entry, as, "*note, –4*. In *change (one's) note*, to tell a (very) different story: late C17–20: coll. till ca. 1850, then S. E. Ex modulated singing. Cf. synon. *change one's tune.*" The explanation is that this expression was heard first in the latter part of the seventeenth century and has continued to be used in the twentieth century. It was considered a colloquial expression until about 1850, at which time it was accepted as standard English. It was derived from the practice of modulated singing.

   Look at several entries to learn to interpret each abbreviation and symbol. As you browse through this detailed, fascinating book, notice the range of quotations and the many sources used.

2. The appendix has an additional, interesting listing of slang words and sources, as *Australian slang*, the expressions *o.k., rhubarb,* and *jazz terms.*

PE
1580
S5

AN ETYMOLOGICAL DICTIONARY OF THE ENGLISH LANGUAGE, New ed., revised and enlarged
By Walter William Skeat
Oxford, Clarendon Press, 1910. 780p.

This is a scholarly and venerable work held in high critical regard and known for generations as "Skeat's." Although the section entitled "Brief Notes upon the Languages Cited in the Dictionary," pp. xviii–xxvii, might intimidate one with little knowledge of foreign languages, even a novice scholar can use this volume.

1. Trace the history of the words *surf* and *random*. Another interesting word to examine is *mess*. After reading the entry, look in other dictionaries to see if you can learn when the American meaning of *mess-hall* came into our language.

2. Compare the entries for *lounge* and *psalm* with those in the *Oxford Dictionary of English Etymology*. What do you consider the notable differences to be?

3. The appendix is an important section. Notice the helpful lists of homonyms, prefixes, and suffixes.

There is an abridged edition with abbreviated etymologies, explanations, and quotations, which retains the useful listings in the appendix, titled *A Concise Etymological Dictionary of the English Language* (new and corrected impr., Oxford, Clarendon Press, 1911, xvi, 664p., repr. 1978).

PE
2846
C46

NEW DICTIONARY OF AMERICAN SLANG
Edited by Robert L. Chapman
N.Y., Harper & Row, 1986. xxxvi, 485p.

This work is based on the *Dictionary of American Slang* (N.Y., Thomas Y. Crowell, 1960, 1967, 1975), compiled by Harold Wentworth and Stuart Berg Flexner, which is credited as being "the first full-scale dictionary of American slang." The editor provides a history of slang and explains the background and plan of the dictionary in the preface. The preface to the first edition is included, and gives a very interesting description of the changes in, and the types or levels of, the English language.

1. Read the section "Guide to the Dictionary." Since the words defined are slang, note the explanation of "impact symbols".

2. Look up *crib*. The numbered entries give parts of speech, usage examples, dating and provenience labels. Synonyms are indicated by an equal sign.

   When usage examples are provided, full bibliographic information is not given. See *hooked* and *hacker.*

3. In the entry for *chow down*, what do the abbreviations *v phr fr* stand for?

4. If you have wondered how commonly used expressions change in meaning, read the entries for *hard hat* and *lucked out.*

   This dictionary is a valuable, frequently used reference source.

PE
1580
O5

**OXFORD DICTIONARY OF
ENGLISH ETYMOLOGY**
Edited by C. T. Onions with the assistance of
G. W. S. Friedrichsen and R. W. Burchfield
Oxford, Clarendon Press, 1966. 1,025p.

The editor of this dictionary was one of the coeditors of the *Oxford English Dictionary,* and thus eminently qualified to prepare this etymological work. As the publisher's note indicates, Onions died before the dictionary was printed, but he had completed the major part of it—the planning and most of the entries.

A review at the time of publication stated that the dictionary's "24,000 main entries and about 14,000 derivatives are based on the *Oxford English Dictionary,* but brought up to date with recent research. Pronunciation, present day meaning, and its earliest form in written English are given for each entry. Some words of U.S. origin are included, as well as both personal and geographical names. . . . The excellence of the dictionary's content and the authority of its compiler will make this volume useful in college and public libraries" (*Wilson Library Bulletin,* Nov. 1966, p. 339).

1. The introduction is of interest to a student of linguistics and to anyone fascinated by the development of language. You must read the section in the introduction on order and arrangement of articles to be able to use the dictionary efficiently. The key to pronunciation and the section on interpretation of abbreviations are equally important.

2. To gain confidence in using this book, read the entry for *friend*. You will find that you will have to keep referring to the abbreviations key in the front of the book. After the first meaning given, there is a (J.). There you will find that (J.) indicates the meaning is credited to (Dr. S.) Johnson. After the (J.) there is a "selection of the senses in order to illustrate the general trend of the sense-development" (as explained in the introduction, p. x). The first of these is *lover*, preceded by the symbol for obsolete and followed by OE (Old English). From this you can follow the history of the word.

3. An interesting, rather amusing, and easy to interpret entry is *ignoramus*. As an example of a very detailed, scholarly analysis, turn to *er suffix*.

OXFORD ENGLISH DICTIONARY
Being a corrected re-issue, with an Introduction, Supplement, and Bibliography, of a New English Dictionary on Historical Principles; founded mainly on the materials collected by the Philological Society. Edited by James A. H. Murray, Henry Bradley, W. A. Craigie, and C. T. Onions
Oxford, Clarendon Press, 1933 (reprinted 1961).
13 v. and supplement

The *Oxford English Dictionary*, or *OED*, is the most monumental and respected of all English-language dictionaries. Many years in the making, this dictionary was produced by eminent philological scholars who piloted it from its creation to its final completion. The planning for the dictionary began in 1857, and "the last page of it was passed to press in 1928."

"The aim of this dictionary is to present in alphabetical series the words that have formed the English vocabulary from the time of earliest records down to the present day, with all the relevant facts concerning their form, sense, history, pronunciation, and etymology" (Preface). The editors traced the history of each word, citing by date its first appearance in print and recording subsequent changes. The meanings and usage of each word are illustrated by completely documented literary quotations. It is stated in the preface that 1,800,000 quotations are actually printed, and also that "there is no aspect of English linguistic history that the Dictionary has not illuminated."

1. The historical introduction in volume 1 describes in detail the planning and dedicated work of the editors and their large staff.

   At least scan the section titled General Explanations, and study those parts you find necessary to understand the entries. You might find yourself caught up in the explanations, such as this one concerning pronunciation: "The pronunciation is the actual living form or forms of a word, that is, *the word itself,* of which the current spelling is only a symbolization . . ." (p. xxxiv).

   The sections titled "Key to Pronunciation," "List of Abbreviations," and "Signs" follow "General Explanations."

2. Look up the word *business.* In the three columns given to this word, note the number and variety of quotations, which show the changes in meaning.

   Banana is an interesting entry for demonstrating how much information is available through tracing the use of a word.

3. If on looking up *heroism* you wanted a complete citation of the source for the quotation from Bentham, "Acts of heroism are in the very essence of them but rare . . .," you would find it in "List of Books Quoted in the Oxford English Dictionary," which is in the back of the last volume, volume 13. This impressive bibliography is more than eighty three-column pages long. Many American authors are included, such as Hawthorne, Thoreau, and Woodrow Wilson.

PE
1625
M53

A SUPPLEMENT TO THE OXFORD ENGLISH DICTIONARY
Edited by R. W. Burchfield
Oxford, Clarendon Press. V. 1, A–G, 1972; v. 2, H–N, 1976; v. 3, O–Scz, 1982; v. 4, Se–Z, 1986

The *Supplement,* in four volumes, follows the same format as the original set of the *OED,* but contains words that have come into the vocabulary of the English-speaking world from 1884 to the present.

The work continues the tradition of scholarship and comprehensiveness, and reviews have assessed it as a magnificent achievement.

There is an unusual graphic analysis of the editorial process on page xvi of volume 1. The preface reveals the change in philosophy from the days of Dr. Johnson, who would admit "no testimony of living authors." The editor states that "my colleagues and I . . . do not personally approve of all the words and phrases that are recorded in this dictionary nor necessarily condone their use by others. Nevertheless . . . we have set them all down as objectively as possible to form a permanent record of the language of our time, the useful and the neutral, those that are decorous and well-formed, beside those that are controversial, tasteless, or worse" (Preface, v. 2, p. viii). Language, with its attributes of complexity, change, and mobility, reflects society itself. The *Supplement* keeps pace with the times and adds the richness of contemporary thought and language to the historically valuable parent work.

1. In glancing through the first volume, one is soon aware of the number of U.S. word origins. The word *boost* is labeled "colloq. (orig. U.S.)." The expression *cliff-hanger* is another U.S. original. The history of the term *McCarthyism* is documented with quotations from various sources.

2. There is an extraordinary coverage of medical, scientific, and technical terms.

3. In contrast, there are some possibly unexpected entries, such as *hullo*, which includes an amusing selection of quotations.

4. As an example of the very detailed scholarship to be found, turn to the article on the prefix *non*.

5. Read the entries for several words that are not a part of your present vocabulary. One can become wholly absorbed in this *OED Supplement*!

<table>
<tr><td>PE
1625
R3</td><td>**THE RANDOM HOUSE DICTIONARY OF THE
ENGLISH LANGUAGE, 2d ed., unabridged**
Stuart Berg Flexner, Editor-in-Chief
N.Y., Random House, 1987. xlii, 2,478, 32p. il.</td></tr>
</table>

In the preface to the second edition, the editor states that "the overriding purpose of this Second Edition is threefold: (1) to provide the user with an accurate, accessible guide to the meanings, spellings, pronunciations, usage, and history of the words in our language . . . ; (2) to provide a scrupulously up-to-date dictionary of record, a storehouse and mirror of the language . . . ; (3) to bring to the user the results of the most recent, authoritative research and knowledge from scholars and experts in all fields, edited with care" (p. viii).

At the beginning of the dictionary, there are essays on the history of the English language, usage, dialects, and the pronunciation of American English. These are followed by the section "How to Use the Random House Dictionary." Explanations with examples are given for all parts of the dictionary entries. Look carefully through these instructions. The next sections cover sound-spelling correspondences in English, abbreviations used in the definitions, pronunciation and etymology keys.

1. In the entries, the most frequently used meanings are given first, with archaic and obsolete meanings last. The entries include biographical and geographical names and titles of literary and artistic works.

   At the bottom of every left-hand page, there is a concise etymology key; at the bottom of every right-hand page is a concise pronunciation key.

2. As an example of words with multiple meanings, see the numbered definitions of *play*, and the synonym list; for geographical names, look up *Rio Bravo* and the cross reference to "(def. 1)" of *Rio Grande*; for the date of first use of a term, see *trade edition*.

3. At the end of the dictionary are sections on signs and symbols; a directory of colleges and universities; the *Declaration of Independence* and the *Constitution of the United States*; concise dictionaries of French, Spanish, Italian and German; a manual of style; and an atlas of the world.

PE
1630
B3

THE SECOND BARNHART DICTIONARY OF NEW ENGLISH
Edited by Clarence L. Barnhart, Sol Steinmetz, and Robert K. Barnhart
Bronxville, N.Y., Barnhart/Harper & Row, 1980. xv, 520p.

The editors describe this dictionary as "a supplement to existing general purpose, English-language dictionaries" and "a continuation of the first *Barnhart Dictionary of New English* issued in 1973." They advise that the two works "contain more than 10,000 words and meanings not entered or inadequately explained in standard dictionaries and were designed "to make an up-to-date and accurate record of standard English" (p. v, vi).

Following the table of contents there is a list of language notes. Read several of these to see what is offered in addition to the alphabetized entries.

The main entries include parts of speech, meanings, usage labels, notes, and quotations to show usage and "the environment in which a word is used." Etymologies are given wherever appropriate, and the year of earliest available evidence for use of a word or meaning is indicated in brackets. Pronunciation is given for difficult words.

1. It is fun and fruitful to turn pages at random to learn the scope of the entries. It is difficult to think of any area of contemporary interest that is not represented. See *Archie Bunker, xerography* (extended sense), *access, structural unemployment, vitamin B17, acid rain, Ultrasuede, Las Vegas line, Pin-yin,* and *go down the tube.*

2. As an example of the numerous cross-references in many entries, see *Delaney amendment;* as an instance of the usage notes, see *benign neglect.*

PE
1625
L53

THE SHORTER OXFORD ENGLISH DICTIONARY ON HISTORICAL PRINCIPLES, 3d ed.
Prepared by William Little, H. W. Fowler, and Jessie Coulson; revised and edited by C. T. Onions; completely reset with etymologies revised by G. W. S. Friedrichsen. With revised addenda
Oxford, Clarendon Press, 1985. 2v.

We learn from the preface that an abridged form of the *Oxford English Dictionary* (q.v.) was envisioned from the outset by the creators of the *OED*. "The aim of this Dictionary is to present in miniature all the features of the principal work" (Preface to the First Edition).

The introduction explains the essential characteristics, arrangement, symbols, and abbreviations. As in the *OED*, the earliest-known occurrence of each word and meaning is indicated. Meanings, quotations, and authorities are given chronologically.

1. Look up *arm*. Note that the meanings are divided by groups under Roman numerals, then divided under Arabic figures, with illustrative quotations.

   Read the entries for *develop* and *flute*, plus a few others, so that you can more easily work with this valued dictionary.
2. There is a list of authors and books cited (p. xvi–xxii).

   The addenda at the end of volume 2 includes words that appear in the *Supplement to the Oxford English Dictionary* (q.v.).

PE
1630
A17

12,000 WORDS: A SUPPLEMENT TO WEBSTER'S THIRD NEW INTERNATIONAL DICTIONARY
Springfield, Mass., Merriam-Webster, 1986. 24a, 212p.

"A dictionary begins to go out-of-date as soon as it is published. When Webster's Third New International Dictionary appeared in 1961, it provided as complete a coverage of contemporary American English as was then available" (Preface). Since 1966, an addenda section has been added every five years to record the changes and additions to the living language. "12,000 Words is simply the most recent Addenda Section of Webster's Third New International Dictionary" (Preface).

In the preface, the editors stress the need to learn how to use a dictionary. Refer to the explanatory notes in the front of the book, which explain how to interpret each entry. You will find the following section on "The Recent Growth of English Vocabulary" a very interesting, informative, and frequently humorous background on where the new words come from, how they are formed, and how they get into Merriam-Webster dictionaries.

1. "Abbreviations and symbols are included as main entries in the vocabulary" (p. 16a). This also applies to acronyms. Look up PC, PG-13, AIDS, ESOP, and MIRV.

2. In the entry for *transformation**n 1, what does the cross reference *in the Dict.* refer to? What does the asterisk indicate?

   Note the illustrative quotations following many definitions, as for *critical mass*.

3. As examples of new words in our language, you will find *bag lady* and *gridlock*. Look for the abundant number of words from science, medicine, cookery, and sports, and the inclusion of slang and current popular expressions.

PE
1628
W5633

**WEBSTER'S NEW WORLD DICTIONARY OF
AMERICAN ENGLISH, 3d college ed.**
Victoria Neufeldt, Editor-in-Chief;
David B. Guralnik, Editor-in-Chief Emeritus
N.Y., Webster's New World, 1988. xxvi, 1,574p. il.

The editor-in-chief emeritus, David B. Guralnik, states in his historical overview that this dictionary has been written to "once and for all scotch Ambrose Bierce's definition of *dictionary* as 'a malevolent device for cramping the growth of a language and making it hard and inelastic'" (p. x). The aim has been to make each edition a reflection of its time.

Essays on the English language and on etymology precede the text.

1. All main entries are in strict alphabetical order. Refer to the guide to the use of the dictionary. Examples are given with explanations of the entries. Etymology is a strong feature of this dictionary: "Etymologies appear in entry blocks inside open double brackets that make them clearly distinguishable in their position before the definitions proper" (p. xiv). The senses are in historical order, with the most recent use given last.

2. Look up: (1) *degree* (Note the field labels used to clarify the application of use, as education, law, math, music, etc.); (2) *laser* (Were you aware of the etymology as shown within the open double brackets? What is the purpose of the open star symbol before the entry?); (3) *Sutter's Mill* and *Laurence Olivier* (examples of entries for geographical and biographical names); (4) *VCR* (After the abbreviation, the term *videocassette recorder* is printed in small capitals. What does that indicate?)

3. At the end of the dictionary, there is a chart of the Indo-European Family of Languages, and sections on editorial style and special signs and symbols.

PE
1628
W5638

**WEBSTER'S NINTH NEW
COLLEGIATE DICTIONARY**
Springfield, Mass., Merriam-Webster, 1987. 1,563p.

"Webster's Ninth New Collegiate Dictionary is the latest in the Collegiate line of Merriam-Webster dictionaries which began in 1898" and is a completely new edition, "meant to serve the general public as its chief source of information about the words of our language"

(Preface). The information given is based on the publisher's collection of citations, which, at the time of this edition, numbered 13 million.

Look carefully at the section on explanatory notes, which includes a chart with a detailed analysis of entries and page references to explanations. This is followed by guides to the entries, pronunciation, an essay on the English language in the dictionary, abbreviations, and pronunciation symbols.

At the back of the book you will find listings of abbreviations and symbols for chemical elements, foreign words and phrases, biographical and geographical names, colleges and universities of the United States and Canada, a handbook of style, and an index.

In this edition, "two features make their first appearance in any Merriam-Webster dictionary. Before the first entered sense of each entry for a generic word, the user of this Collegiate will find a date that indicates when the earliest example known to us of the use of that sense was written or printed," and "a number of entries for words posing special problems of confused or disputed usage include for the first time brief articles that provide the dictionary user with suitable guidance on the usage in question" (Preface). The word *aggravate* is provided as an example of the latter feature, entered on page 19 under *usage paragraphs*.

The main entries are in alphabetical order, letter by letter. Review your understanding of this alphabetizing method by looking up *North Star*.

The order of senses is historical, with the senses in contemporary use listed last.

1. "The treatment of synonymy has been completely revised for this edition so that all the synonym articles now discriminate from one another words of closely associated meaning" (Preface). Read the entries for *function* and *quality*. What is indicated when words are printed in small capitals? Note the illustrative quotations used for *quality*.

2. You would assume that *microcomputer* is a recent addition to our language, but would you be surprised at the dates of first written or printed use of *astronaut* and *coffee break*?

3. If asked by readers, could you: interpret the etymology of *horn*; pronounce *Thucydides*; explain what "(14c)" refers to in the entry for *delicate*? If you are uncertain about these, refer again to the explanatory notes. Remember, the back matter of the dictionary

includes the pronunciation of biographical and geographical names.

This collegiate dictionary is a respected, standard work used by librarians for ready reference because of its excellent, long-standing reputation and convenient size.

PE
1625
W36

WEBSTER'S THIRD NEW INTERNATIONAL DICTIONARY OF THE ENGLISH LANGUAGE, Unabridged
Editor-in-Chief, Philip Babcock Gove and the Merriam-Webster Editorial Staff
Springfield, Mass., Merriam-Webster, 1986.
110a, 2,662p. il.

Webster's Third is the most respected American unabridged dictionary. The preface describes the philosophy that shaped this edition and the background of its preparation: "In continuation of Merriam-Webster policy the editors of this new edition have held steadfastly to the three cardinal virtues of dictionary making: accuracy, clearness, and comprehensiveness. Whenever these qualities are at odds with each other, accuracy is put first and foremost, for without accuracy there could be no appeal to *Webster's Third New International* as an authority" (p. 4a). Note the academic and professional backgrounds of the editorial staff and outside consultants.

The arrangement is alphabetical, letter by letter. "In definitions of words of many meanings, the earliest ascertainable meaning is given first" (p. 4a). The etymologies are set apart in square brackets.

Look carefully at the table of contents on page 3a. It is helpful to keep in mind for later reference that there is an explanatory chart on page 13a. This is linked to the explanatory notes on the following pages, which provide detailed information about main entries, pronunciation, etymology, usage notes, and run-on entries to enable you to understand the information contained in each entry.

The pronunciation guide may seem overwhelming. Look through it thoroughly enough to be able to recall available scholarly research that might be needed to answer an inquiry. "The edition shows as far as possible the pronunciations prevailing in general cultivated conversational usage, both formal and informal, throughout the English-speaking world. It does not attempt to dictate what that usage should be." (p. 4a).

"A large number of verbal illustrations mostly from the mid-twentieth century has been woven into the defining pattern with a view of contributing considerably to the user's interest and understanding by showing a word used in context. . . . More than 14,000 different authors are quoted" (p. 4a). Complete citations for the quotations are not given.

1. An addenda to update the dictionary has been included every five years since the 1966 edition. See the evidence for updating in the entries for *AIDS, word processing, ayatollah,* and *genetic counseling.*

2. To test what you have learned in the guides for use of this unabridged dictionary, study the entry for *habit.* Note its etymology; the chronological listing of meanings; its rare, obsolete, and special meanings; and the quotations and cross-references.

   Look up that overworked word *pejorative.* Could you explain the pronunciation as indicated?

   As an example of the medical and scientific terms included, look at the concise definition and illustration of *heart.* Locate entries in the nuclear and space sciences.

3. Skim the entry for *clear* for the fascinating variety of quotations—from novelists, poets, a philosopher, and a Supreme Court justice—clarifying the different meanings. Note that synonyms are listed in small capitals.

4. Geographical and biographical names are not included. Separate Merriam-Webster dictionaries have been published with more comprehensive coverage of those areas than would be feasible in this dictionary.

   Special features in *Webster's Third* include the section entitled "Forms of Address," which has an unusually complete list of positions and titles, and the many tables throughout the text, such as those on numbers, geologic time, and formations. There is a brief biography of Noah Webster at the end of the book, including a history of his *American Dictionary.*

5. Did you notice the insignia on *Webster's Third?* It marks what is considered the true "Webster's," published by the Merriam-Webster Company. The use of the name *Webster* in the titles of other dictionaries has often confused those referring to or purchasing a dictionary.

CHILDREN'S AND YOUNG ADULT SOURCES

WEBSTER'S ELEMENTARY DICTIONARY
Springfield, Mass., Merriam-Webster, 1986.
20a, 587p. il.

This Merriam-Webster dictionary was written for students in the elementary grades. Words are selected on the basis of their appearance in school textbooks and other materials, and on studies of words used by children in this age group.

The colorful binding with its color illustrations of words found in the dictionary should attract young people and assure them that not all is dull and forbidding inside a dictionary.

1. In the section entitled "Key to Using Your Dictionary," each part of a sample entry is named and set in a bright color to form a color-keyed guide. On the following pages, entitled "Using Your Dictionary," the terms are fully explained, with examples keyed in the same color. As you read this section, remember that the explanations are intended for students in the elementary grades.

    The lists of abbreviations and pronunciation symbols immediately precede the text. Notice the type size and spacing designed for young readers.

2. Pronunciation is placed between slant lines after each entry. Keys to the symbols are on the bottom right corners of odd-numbered pages.

    Synonyms are written in small capital letters. These are also cross-references to separate entries that provide full explanations of the meaning or use. At the end of some entries you will find indented "synonym paragraphs"—discussions, or verbal illustrations—of the synonyms to clarify the differences between them. As an example, see ¹*model*. What does the "1" indicate?

3. Word histories are set apart by the color blue. Many of them are made interesting through a story-telling style, such as those for *canary* and *éclair*.

4. Color illustrations are placed throughout the text. Compare the illustrations in *Webster's Elementary Dictionary* with those in the *World Book Dictionary* and the *Webster's New World Dictionary for Young Readers*. Are the subjects well chosen? Do they add to

an understanding of the meanings? Are the illustrations placed next to or near the entries?

5. At the end of the book there are lists of abbreviations in general use, signs and symbols, presidents and vice-presidents of the United States, and geographical names (states of the United States, provinces of Canada, and nations of the world, with their capitals and pronunciations given).

PE
1625
W73

THE WORLD BOOK DICTIONARY
A Thorndike-Barnhart Dictionary
Edited by Clarence L. Barnhart and
Robert K. Barnhart
Chicago, World Book, 1988. 2v. il.

The World Book Dictionary, first published in 1963, is singularly impressive in its format. The large two-volume set is the most comprehensive of the respected Thorndike-Barnhart school dictionaries, and is designed to supplement the *World Book Encyclopedia.* In addition to the continuous revision of the dictionary, there is a special supplement in each annual edition of the *World Book Year Book* listing new words and meanings of that year. "From its inception, *The World Book Dictionary* has aimed to be useful to all members of the family and to students of various ages" (p. 5).

The two volumes (A–K, L–Z) are arranged in alphabetical order, letter by letter. There are 124 pages of supplementary educational material at the beginning of volume 1, including articles on where English comes from; making words, which has a two-page listing of prefixes, suffixes, and combining forms; learning to spell correctly; and punctuation. Note the section on increasing your word power (p. 39), which has graded vocabulary inventories, or exercises, for third grade through college. These sections are followed by information on how to write effectively, including preparation of term papers, manuscripts, and letters; using different languages; metric conversion tables; and lists of first names with their derivations and meanings.

The editors stress what *Reference Readiness* emphasizes for all reference works: read the introduction and guide to the use of the book. "All dictionaries are not alike. Words, definitions, and etymologies may be arranged in different ways in different dictionaries. The use of terms and symbols may vary" (p. 113). It is recommended that you read the section on using this dictionary, which begins on page 113.

1. Because it complements the *World Book Encyclopedia*, the dictionary does not contain biographical and geographical information. It does identify figures of legend and mythology, as Tristram and Athena.

2. Look up *case*. Main entries are in boldface type, extending into the margin. Vertical lines appear between syllables. The pronunciation is given in parentheses. If more than one pronunciation is listed, the preferred is given first. The part of speech follows, then the numbered meanings, with the most commonly used meaning first. Note the illustrative sentences and phrases provided to clarify the meanings; the provision of synonyms; and the etymology in square brackets at the end of the entry.

   There is a pronunciation key at the bottom right corner of each odd-numbered page.

3. Preferred forms of words with variant spellings are shown with an equal sign. The preferred form is the main entry. See *assimilatory* as an example. Slang is given full coverage, as represented by the entry for *dope*, with its multiple meanings.

4. The editors state that there are more than three thousand illustrations to extend and clarify the definitions. Only line drawings are used; there are no illustrations in color. Remember that illustrated entries are marked with an asterisk, as those for *cradle*, *drum*, and *germanium*.

MEDICAL DICTIONARIES

Reference librarians in public libraries are frequently asked, usually by telephone, for the spelling or definition of a medical term not found in a standard or home-use dictionary. There are many medical dictionaries available with simplified to professional and scientific terminology, from abridged to comprehensive editions, and these should be evaluated for authority, accuracy, and other criteria as for standard dictionaries. The following are a few of the established titles usable for ready reference:

Dorland's Illustrated Medical Dictionary, 26th ed. Philadelphia, Saunders, 1981.
Illustrated Stedman's Medical Dictionary, 24th ed. Baltimore, Williams and Wilkins, 1982.

Taber's Cyclopedic Medical Dictionary, 15th ed. Edited by Clayton L. Thomas. Philadelphia, Davis, 1985.

Webster's New World/Stedman's Concise Medical Dictionary. N.Y., Webster's New World, 1987. Abridged edition of *Illustrated Stedman's Medical Dictionary,* 1982.

1. Compare the accessibility and clarity of entries in several of these dictionaries by looking up the names of syndromes. In one medical dictionary, a specific syndrome might have a separate entry with an informative definition; in another, after the syndrome name, you might find a *see* reference to *syndromes,* where there will be a listing with one-sentence definitions for those selected for inclusion.

   It is recommended you learn the differences in the format and content of these sources.

THE THESAURUS

A thesaurus is a book of words and their synonyms and antonyms. The most famous of these is by Peter Mark Roget, whose *Thesaurus of English Words and Phrases, Classified and Arranged so as to facilitate the Expressions of Ideas and Assist in Literary Composition* was published over one hundred years ago.

In 1805, when Roget, a prominent physician and university professor, began his compilation of words and phrases, he planned it only for his own use. He invented an ingenious scheme of grouping words and phrases according to ideas instead of alphabetically as in a dictionary. This system of categorizing ideas is the key to the popularity and long life of his work. It was an immediate success when published in 1852, and has retained its usefulness to writers and speakers through many revised editions.

In 1910, C. O. Sylvester Mawson presented a modification of Roget's system, which used a simpler and more practical scheme. His thesaurus was arranged in alphabetical order, eliminating the need for the index necessary in the original work.

Subsequently, other notable thesauri have been published. You should be familiar with their varied formats. Selected examples are examined here.

ROGET'S THESAURUS OF THE ENGLISH LANGUAGE IN DICTIONARY FORM
Being a presentation of Roget's Thesaurus of English Words and Phrases in a modernized, more complete and more convenient dictionary form with an Appendix of Foreign Words and Expressions
By Christopher Orlando Sylvester Mawson
Garden City, N.Y., Garden City Publishing, 1931. 600p.

After considerable experimentation with the original Roget work, C. O. Sylvester Mawson devised the first alphabetically arranged thesaurus. In the preface he says: "The present volume retains the practical advantages of the standardized Thesaurus without the disadvantages. . . . The old Roget lists are here, modernized, refurbished, and rearranged; but there is one striking difference: every meaning is covered under one head" (p. v).

To see the arrangement of the listings and the treatment of words, *animal*, *ornament*, and *regularity* are interesting examples in this pioneer work.

ROGET'S INTERNATIONAL THESAURUS, 4th ed.
Revised by Robert L. Chapman
N.Y., Thomas Y. Crowell, 1977. xxiv, 1,316p.

This edition, as those preceding it, has been "compiled according to the plan devised originally by Peter Mark Roget." Words are arranged in categories by their meanings, and there is a comprehensive index. Read the introductory guide.

"The search for a word that you need is a simple, two-step process, which begins in the index" (p. ix). Look up a word in the index, where you will find the subentry closest to the meaning you want. Follow the number cited after the subentry into the text, and you will find a group of words with similar meanings. The index, which takes up about half the book, is an integral part of the scheme and must always be consulted first.

Remember that this thesaurus is a grouping of words according to ideas. On page xvii there is a section entitled "Synopsis of Categories," which is helpful for understanding the text.

1. Turn to the detailed listing of terms designating narcotics. Is the word *narcotic* in the index? If you looked up a specific type of

narcotic, would you find the reference to the subentries 687.52–.53?

2. As additional examples of categories with lists of associated words, look in the index under *proper thing,* with the subentries *custom* 642.1 and *moral rightness* 958.1; check the listings under *manners of cooking,* and under *radiation and radioactivity.*

Once Roget's unique system is learned, the book is fun to use. Although the system is complicated, it offers users a vast and varied treasury of words and phrases.

PE   **ROGET'S II: THE NEW THESAURUS,**
1591   **expanded ed.**
R715   **By the Editors of the *American Heritage Dictionary***
Boston, Houghton Mifflin, 1988. xvi, 1,135p.

The editors state that *Roget's II* is an entirely new work and "represents a significant change from traditional thesaurus making" (Preface). Read the preface, introduction, and the essential section entitled "How to Use This Book."

"In the left-hand column of each page, all entries are arranged in alphabetical order and are classified by part of speech. Every word is accurately defined. . . . Sentences and phrases using the entry words in context provide guidance in usage. In the right-hand column, synonyms, idioms, near-synonyms, near-antonyms, and antonyms are listed alphabetically within groups and are presented adjacent to each defined meaning of each discrete sense" (Preface).

1. The editors claim that "since *Roget's II* defines all entry words and their corresponding synonyms, the work is self-contained. Therefore, the user does not need to verify a meaning by consulting a dictionary" (Preface). Test this assumption by looking up the word *adore* in a standard dictionary. Note the meanings and examples of proper usage. Then turn to *Roget's II* to *adore verb.* On page 610, the entry *love verb* has two meanings, each with a cross-reference to the main entry *adore.* If your search began with the task of helping a reader select an appropriate synonym for the verb *love,* would you find any difficulty with this listing?

A good example of the editors' intentions as expressed in the preface can be found in the entry for *myth.*

2. Patrons frequently ask reference librarians about slang. In this thesaurus, the entry *total verb* has, as sense number 3, "To cause the complete ruin or wreckage of," with a cross-reference to the main entry, *destroy.* The synonyms for the first meaning of *destroy* include *total.* The label *slang* is not used. Compare this with the entry in a standard dictionary or in the *Dictionary of Slang and Unconventional English* (q.v.).

3. For the entry *accord verb,* sense number 4, the right-hand column lists *grant verb.* Why was the part of speech added there and not to the three numbered entries above it? For *cast noun,* sense number 5, you are given a cross-reference to *kind²*. What does the "2" indicate? For *paucity noun,* the right-hand column shows *shortage* in small capitals. Is this a cross-reference?

The type and format of this thesaurus make each entry stand out, and makes possible quick and easy location of main entries and their meanings and synonyms.

<table>
<tr><td>PE</td><td rowspan="3">**WEBSTER'S COLLEGIATE THESAURUS**
Springfield, Mass., Merriam-Webster, 1988. 26a, 868p.</td></tr>
<tr><td>1591</td></tr>
<tr><td>W38</td></tr>
</table>

PE
1591
W38

WEBSTER'S COLLEGIATE THESAURUS
Springfield, Mass., Merriam-Webster, 1988. 26a, 868p.

In the preface, the editor answers the question: "What does the user look for in a thesaurus? . . . he is seeking a more appropriate term than the one he has in mind." The introduction gives an interesting and readable history of the evolution of the Thesaurus, which traces the modern concept of a collection of synonyms to the book, *Synonymous, Etymological, and Pronouncing English Dictionary,* by William Perry, published in 1805—almost fifty years before Roget's famous work.

Webster's Collegiate Thesaurus ranks high among thesauri for its scholarly precision and scope. Instead of presenting words, expressions, and phrases that are synonymous (some only remotely related), as in Roget's work, this thesaurus begins by pinpointing differences in word meanings—the gradations and shades of meanings—and then lists synonyms for each. (Note that among those works that include *Roget* in the title, some do not use the original format and method, such as *Roget's II: The New Thesaurus* (q.v.).

In the introductory section, see the chart and explanations of entries.

Each denotation is numbered. In addition to synonyms, the editors list related words, contrasted words, the true antonym (opposite), and intermediate antonyms. Frequently a sentence or phrase is given to illustrate how a word is used, and almost every entry has a cross-reference that directs the user to another word, with a number indicating its specific meaning. Double bars alert the user to consult a dictionary for fuller meanings.

1. Turn to the entry for *considered: considered adj syn* DELIBERATE 1, advised, aforethought, designed, premeditated . . . *rel* intentional, voluntary, willful . . . *con* impulsive, instinctive, spontaneous . . . *ant* unconsidered.

   Now turn to *deliberate adj.* The first sense offers a statement of the core meaning shared by the synonyms, "arrived at after due thought," and an example phrase is given: [a *deliberate* judgment]. Two synonyms are then listed for the other senses of *deliberate.* The synonyms are in small capitals to indicate that each is treated as a main entry in the alphabetical arrangement of the book.

The *Collegiate Thesaurus* is more sophisticated in its analysis and treatment of words than most of the volumes traditionally based on Roget's work. The listings include contemporary words and usage. The entries for old-fashioned terms are fun to read, such as the one for *Sunday best.* Slang and vulgarisms are included, as they are in *Webster's Third* (q.v.).

PE
1591
W39

WEBSTER'S NEW DICTIONARY OF SYNONYMS:
A Dictionary of Discriminated Synonyms with Antonyms and Analogous and Contrasted Words
Springfield, Mass., Merriam-Webster, 1984. 32a, 909p.

The purposes of this book as stated in the preface are to provide a means of making clear comparisons between words of common denotation; to enable readers to distinguish the differences in implications, connotations, and applications among such words; and to assist in choosing precisely suited words for a purpose.

The introductory matter includes sections entitled "A Survey of the History of English Synonymy," "Synonym: Analysis and Definition," and "The Treatment of Antonyms and Analogous and Contrasted Words." The explanatory notes, which immediately precede the alphabetical listing, should be studied. All the principal devices used in the dictionary are clearly explained.

1. Read the entries for *fragrance, eager,* and *journey.*
   There are multiple usage examples and quotations from named authors or sources. The complete citations for the quotations are not given. At the end of the book there is a list of authors quoted.
2. Find a few synonyms of which the distinctions as provided by this dictionary would be useful to a patron seeking precise meanings of words. Some examples are *face* and *countenance* and *empty* and *vacant.* Under *grace* there are two distinct meanings: (1) mercy or charity, and (2) elegance or dignity. In each group there is one word preceded by an asterisk. How would you explain this to a student?

Librarians are frequently called on to write reviews or annotations of books, just as they are frequently asked to speak about books. In either situation, the librarian whose vocabulary is extensive, precise, and vivid can communicate most effectively. This dictionary can help each of us become more proficient in the use of our language.

PE   **WEBSTER'S SCHOOL THESAURUS**
1591   Springfield, Mass., Merriam-Webster, 1978. 12a, 499p.
W44

"*Webster's School Thesaurus* is especially designed for young people who want to enlarge their vocabulary and acquaint themselves with the rich variety of the English language . . . [and] is offered as a reference book that is close to being an adult tool" (Preface). It is based primarily on *Webster's Third New International Dictionary* (q.v.).
   The thesaurus is described as a "storehouse of useful words" in the English language, which, through the complexity of its make-up, is "peculiarly rich in synonyms" (p. 4a). The editor states that the introduction provides a "discussion on just what makes a word a synonym or an antonym, a related word or a contrasted one," and the explanatory notes that follow "contain an explanation of the way *Webster's School Thesaurus* is organized and discuss the kinds of information which may be found at each entry in the book" (Preface).

1. After reading the explanatory notes, look at the multiple listings under *short, will,* and *wise.* Note the *compare* cross-references,

the *see* references, and the idiomatic equivalents. What do double bars before a word indicate?

2. "This thesaurus is concerned with the general vocabulary of English. Most obsolete and archaic words and highly technical terms have been left out" (p. 7a). Slang and regional expressions are included, as *willy-willy* and *deep-six.*

3. Remember that to find the most appropriate term, the thesaurus should be used along with an adequate dictionary. This can be demonstrated by the many synonyms provided for "dark *adj* 1," which include *caliginous* and *murky.* Would you use either of these words as a synonym for "dark" to describe a person's shadow without first looking it up in a dictionary?

DICTIONARIES
Additional Titles

Abbreviations Dictionary. Ralph De Sola. Augmented International 7th ed. N.Y., Elsevier, 1986.

Acronyms, Initialisms and Abbreviations Dictionary, 13th ed. Edited by Julie E. Towell. Detroit, Gale Research, 1989. 3v.

American Heritage Dictionary, 2d college ed. Boston, Houghton Mifflin, 1985.

American Heritage Student's Dictionary. Peter Davies, Editor-in-Chief. Boston, Houghton Mifflin, 1986.
For junior high school students.

Dictionary of American Regional English. Frederic G. Cassidy, Chief Editor. Cambridge, Mass., Belknap Press of Harvard University Press, 1985– . In progress.

Dictionary of Foreign Phrases and Abbreviations, 3d ed. Translated and compiled by Kevin Guinagh. N.Y., H. W. Wilson, 1982.

Harper Dictionary of Foreign Terms, 3d ed. Edited by Eugene Ehrlich. N.Y., Harper & Row, 1987. Revised edition of C. O. Sylvester Mawson's *Dictionary of Foreign Terms;* 2d ed. Revised by Charles Berlitz; now includes an English index to the foreign terms.

Macmillan Dictionary for Children. William D. Halsey, Editor. N.Y., Macmillan, 1987.
For students ages 7 through 11.

Morris Dictionary of Word and Phrase Origins, 2d ed. By William and Mary Morris. N.Y., Harper & Row, 1988.

Oxford-Duden Pictorial English Dictionary. Edited by John Pheby. Oxford and N.Y., Oxford University Press, 1981.

"Over 28,000 objects" named and illustrated, with index. Bilingual editions also published in Spanish, French, German, and others.

The Right Word II: A Concise Thesaurus. Boston, Houghton Mifflin, 1983.

For junior high grades and up.

Scott, Foresman Beginning Dictionary. By E. L. Thorndike and Clarence L. Barnhart. Garden City, N.Y., Doubleday, 1983.

Webster's Guide to Abbreviations. Springfield, Mass., Merriam-Webster, 1985.

Webster's New World Dictionary, student ed. David B. Guralnik, Editor-in-Chief. N.Y., Simon and Schuster, 1981.

Webster's New World Thesaurus. Prepared by Charlton Laird, updated by William D. Lutz. N.Y., Webster's New World, 1985.

Webster's School Dictionary. Springfield, Mass., Merriam-Webster, 1986.

Written for high school students; reviewers find it also suitable for junior high students.

2.
ENCYCLOPEDIAS

The reference librarian must evaluate many aspects of an encyclopedia to determine its reliability and usefulness. All reference books should be examined before purchase. The guidelines for selection listed below can be applied generally to many reference works; however, because encyclopedias form the foundation of most reference collections, and because they are expensive, their purchase becomes a matter of very careful appraisal by the librarian. The following factors should be considered:

Authority. Are those responsible for the work (editors, compilers, authors, and publisher) of recognized competence and experience? Are the contributors identified? Are the articles signed?

Accuracy. If the authority is proved, the accuracy should follow; however, specific items should be checked to test the accuracy of statements and statistics.

Recency. Does the work have a recent copyright date? Are the articles up-to-date? If bibliographies are included, are the titles reasonably recent?

Arrangement. Is the arrangement adequately explained, practical, and easy to follow? Is there an index? Are symbols and abbreviations used in the text clearly explained? Are there cross-references? If there are illustrations, charts, or maps, are they placed in close proximity to the text? Are appendixes, addenda, and other "special features" clearly indicated?

Scope. Do the editors or authors describe the scope? Does the coverage confirm their description? Is the scope so broad that the work merely skims the surface?

Format. What is the quality of the paper, printing and binding? Is the paper free from glare and sufficiently opaque that the printing on the reverse side does not interfere with reading? Is the print large, dark and sharp enough for the user to read it with ease? Is the binding sturdy and attractive? Can the volumes be opened flat? Are the margins ample? Does each page have one, two, or three columns? What is the quality of the illustrations?

Do they enhance or detract from the general appearance? Are the volumes an unwieldy size?

Revision. Do the editors explain the policy for revised editions, supplements, or annuals? Continuous revision, increasingly common for encyclopedias, is a desirable feature.

Style. Is the work suitable for the intended audience? Is the text written in a clear, readable style?

Price. No matter how fine or useful a reference work is, if it appears to be overpriced, the librarian cannot purchase it. The high cost of encyclopedias makes their careful selection imperative.

Frequently, a set of encyclopedias is retailed at various prices, the range of which may be very great indeed. This does not necessarily mean that the most costly one is superior in content; the binding may make the difference. A deluxe binding of simulated white leather may increase the price, whereas a darker buckram binding may sell for much less and be more durable. Another reason for the price differential is the sales practice of "special offers" or "package deals," which may include a free atlas or bookcase, or even another set of books. These, of course, should not influence the librarian's decision.

The Collection. Along with all the foregoing factors, the librarian must consider a work in relation to other works in the collection. Does it merely duplicate something already in the library, or does it fill a real need in the collection? Will it be of greater value than a less-expensive and less-detailed work?

As a reference librarian you should become so familiar with the differences among encyclopedias that you know which one to turn to first for the information needed. Such facility comes only with continuous practice and study. Selected titles are described here and others are cited at the end of the chapter. For information on additional encyclopedias, see the English- and foreign-language listings in the *Guide to Reference Books* (q.v.); the English-language encyclopedias included in *General Reference Books for Adults* and *Reference Books for Young Readers* (q.v.); and the reviews available in professional journals such as *Booklist,* and those cited herein in chapter 6.

DS
102.8
E496

ENCYCLOPAEDIA JUDAICA
N.Y., Macmillan, 1972, 16v. il.

"The Encyclopaedia Judaica is the first Jewish encyclopedia on a major scale to be published for many decades. It represents the cumulation

of years of intensive work by scholars from many parts of the world and provides a comprehensive picture of all aspects of Jewish life and knowledge up to the present day, intended for both the Jewish and non-Jewish reader" (Introduction, p. 1). Read the introduction for the history of Jewish encyclopedias and the fascinating discussion of the massive scale development of this encyclopedia.

1. Volume 1 contains the index, among other features. Immediately after the title page, there is a table of contents that directs you to the varied parts of the volume.
   a. The identifying list of international sponsors, editors, and contributors is more than fifty pages long!
   b. Tables of transliteration rules for the Hebrew, Semitic, Yiddish, Arabic, Greek, and Russian languages are provided.
   c. Supplementary lists include the hundred-year Jewish calendar, 1920–2020, year by year, related to the Gregorian calendar; and a detailed chart of the historical relations of the leading Hasidic dynasties to the present time. Beginning on page 193, you will find an extensive but selective listing of internationally published Hebrew newspapers and periodicals.
   d. A unique feature is the inclusion, on pages 221–271, of black-and-white sketches illustrating the history of "pottery, from the Neolithic Period to the end of the Israelite Period," with facing pages identifying each illustration.
   e. Following the special features, there is a detailed alphabetical index to the entire set. Note the explanation of the abbreviations. There are many cross-references that refer to the index itself. The subjects of articles are printed in capital letters: "ALEXANDRIA (city, Egy.)"; if the subject is only included within an article, it is printed in the usual upper- and lower-case letters: "Alexandria (city, Louis.)," with volume and page numbers cited. All illustrations except portrait photographs are indexed.

2. The articles are signed with initials, which are identified in the index volume. Most articles are followed by bibliographies, although many have only one or two titles.

3. One emphasis is on the biographies of persons from ancient to contemporary times. In some cases the dates and places of birth and death are not given; the editors state that these are sometimes

conjectural and sometimes irrelevant—an explanation that seems to embody both fact and wit.

4. It is integral to the appropriate use and understanding of this encyclopedia to keep in mind the editors' introductory statement—"[It] provides a comprehensive picture of all aspects of Jewish life and knowledge up to the present time." Articles on many subjects are limited in information except as specifically related to the Jewish people. This is apparent in the articles on aeronautics, aviation, and astronautics, and in the article on the city of Los Angeles. In contrast, turn to the entry on "History," which begins, after a chronological outline, with the patriarchs and Exodus and continues to the 1970s, taking up more than 200 pages. On a par with this coverage is the article on the Hebrew alphabet. This encyclopedia, which provides a comprehensive single source on the contemporary history of the Jewish people, presents a lengthy, shattering article on the Holocaust. The article begins with a chronological outline and includes photographs, maps, and an extensive bibliography.

————. *Yearbook.* Jerusalem, Encyclopaedia Judaica, 1973——.
————. *Decennial Book*, 1973–1982; Events of 1972–1981. Jerusalem, Encyclopaedia Judaica, 1982.

AE
5
E333

THE ENCYCLOPEDIA AMERICANA,
international ed.
Danbury, Conn., Grolier, 1989. 30v. illus.

The *Americana,* first published in 1829, is the pioneer of multivolume encylopedias published in the United States. Its appeal is to the young adult and adult. It is written in a readable style with authoritative content. The encyclopedia is traditionally strong in its coverage of U.S. history, geography, and biography, but is international in scope and includes well-received scientific and technical articles.

The articles are arranged alphabetically, word by word. Bibliographies are cited at the end of many articles. Read the preface, which describes the arrangement and special features. This is followed by lists of the *Americana* staff, advisory editors, and contributors.

1. There is a comprehensive index in volume 30 that includes cross-references and references to maps and illustrations. Always consult the index first to be certain of the place or places in which to

look for the information you want! Read the guide to the use of the index, and note the list of abbreviations used in the index.

2. Turn to the long article on the province and city of Quebec, Canada. At the head of the article there is an outline of the contents for direct reference to specific information. Under that is an inset called "information highlights." The descriptive text includes the history, government, people, culture, economy, and special points of interest, with maps, color photos, and a bibliography with English and French titles.

3. The following examples demonstrate the coverage provided in different subject areas. For a topic in science, see the article on space exploration. Note that the article is divided into subdivisions with bibliographies written by different experts. How current are the cited sources for additional information? Would the illustrations add to the reader's interest in or knowledge of the subject? For an overview of the varying length and emphasis of biographies, look up the entries on Alexander the Great, Socrates, John Kenneth Galbraith, Bill "Bojangles" Robinson, George Gershwin, and Barbara Jordan. There are many notable long articles in the *Americana,* as on renaissance art and architecture, the U.S. Civil War, and rugs and carpets. Are the articles signed? If so, what are the academic or other affiliations of the contributors?

Continue with your own comparative analysis of the latest edition of *Collier's Encyclopedia, with Bibliography and Index* (William D. Halsey, Editorial Director; Bernard Johnston, Editor-in-Chief. N.Y., Macmillan Educational Co.).

Remember the evaluative factors for encyclopedias outlined at the beginning of this chapter. Read the preface and the introductory guides to the use of *Collier's.*

Select three subjects in different subject categories; then, using the same subjects, compare the coverage in the *Americana* and in the *New Encyclopaedia Britannica.*

You should also refer to the *Academic American Encyclopedia* (Bernard S. Cayne, Editorial Director; K. Anne Ranson, Editor-in-Chief. Danbury, Connecticut, Grolier). Reviews place this encyclopedia as an excellent current ready-reference source, especially for its articles on science and technology, biography, and subjects of current international interest, and for its generous, excellent illustrations and comprehensive index.

BX
841
N44

NEW CATHOLIC ENCYCLOPEDIA
Prepared by an editorial staff at
the Catholic University of America
N.Y., McGraw-Hill, 1967. 15v. il. maps.

"An International Work of Reference on the Teachings, History, Organization, and Activities of the Catholic Church, and on All Institutions, Religions, Philosophies, and Scientific and Cultural Developments Affecting the Catholic Church from its Beginning to the Present" (from the title page).

From the preface we learn that there are some 17,000 signed articles written by 4,800 scholars and specialists, both Catholic and non-Catholic.

Although concerned with providing complete information on the doctrine, organization, and history of the Catholic Church, the editors broadened the horizons and scope to include sciences, arts, literature, religions, and philosophies that have no direct basis in the Catholic Church. Scholars generally agree that the *New Catholic Encyclopedia* is a great achievement.

1. See the table of contents in volume 15. Following the long list of contributors, there are several explanatory sections on various kinds of abbreviations, including bibliographical, general, and Biblical abbreviations. A note directs the user to still another explanation of the abbreviations in the preface. The guide to using the index on page 235 is short and clear, and should be read by anyone about to consult it for the first time.

   By using the index, can you turn quickly to the article on Pope John XXIII? Do you understand the sequence of the listing of persons named John? If uncertain, reread the paragraph on arrangement on page 235 of the index volume.

2. Look up a subject outside the precepts of the Catholic Church to learn the quality and scope of the coverage. See the article on church architecture with its excellent photographs, floor plans, and diagrams. Within the text of this large subject, many aspects are discussed and described. Each subtopic contains a substantial bibliography.

   The bibliographies appended to the articles are valuable, although many titles cited are now out-of-print.

————. *Supplements.* v. 16 (covering the years 1967–74), 1974; v. 17 (Change in the Church), 1979. Palatine, Ill., Publishers Guild, 1981.

AE
5
E363

THE NEW ENCYCLOPAEDIA BRITANNICA, 15th ed.
Philip W. Goetz, Editor-in-Chief
Chicago, Encyclopaedia Britannica, 1988. 32v. il.

This is the oldest of the modern English encyclopedias. From humble beginnings in Edinburgh, Scotland, in 1768, continuing through many editions for more than one hundred years under the auspices of British companies, it passed into American hands in the early part of the twentieth century. Note that the "ae" form of spelling encyclopaedia is always used and is a trademark of Britannica.

Before you begin to use the *New Encyclopaedia Britannica*, first published in 1974 and heavily revised in 1985, you must be aware that it is unlike any other encyclopedia. A revolutionary change in format divides the *Britannica* into four parts: the *Propaedia* (outline of knowledge); *Micropaedia* (ready reference); *Macropaedia* (knowledge in depth); and the *Index*.

The *Propaedia* is defined as the introductory volume, or "antechamber," to the world of learning that the rest of the encyclopedia aims to encompass. It contains a vast ten-part outline of knowledge, which provides a topical survey of the *Macropaedia*.

The ready-reference function is provided through the *Micropaedia*, which consists of twelve volumes. The articles in this division of the set are generally brief, the length varying with the subjects, with cross-references showing where additional information can be found in both the *Micropaedia* and the *Macropaedia*. The educational function is carried out principally through the seventeen volumes entitled the *Macropaedia*, which contain long scholarly articles about most fields of knowledge and interest.

The following outline may help to clarify the organization:

Propaedia	*Micropaedia*	*Macropaedia*	*Index*
1 volume	12 volumes	17 volumes	2 volumes
Introduction & detailed outline	Ready reference & cross-references	Scholarly articles	

Each section is arranged alphabetically, letter by letter. To help the user distinguish among them, the volumes' spines have panels of different colors.

The *New Britannica* has expanded coverage of international subjects and of the sciences. Articles in the *Macropaedia* are signed with the initials of the contributors, who are identified at the end of the *Propaedia*. Most of the articles in the *Micropaedia* are not signed, but a list of contributors is given.

1. Read the instructions in volume 1 on how to use the *Micropaedia*. Turn to the articles on Italy and on the state of Missouri to learn what information is presented in the "ready reference" volumes. It is important to note in the article on Missouri an inset, which you will find in many other articles, that advises *Consult the Index First.* Compare these articles with those in the *Macropaedia*.

   How do the biographies of Leonardo da Vinci and Thomas Jefferson in the *Micropaedia* differ from those in the *Macropaedia*? Are there cross-references, bibliographies, illustrations? Is there an entry for Desmond Tutu, for Hubert H. Humphrey?

   Make this comparison of coverage on the subject of Christianity. Comparing the *Micropaedia* and *Macropaedia* should enable you to make an appropriate choice based on the kind and amount of information a reader needs.

2. As examples of the comprehensive entries in the *Macropaedia*, see the articles on genetics and heredity and on legal systems; note the extraordinary coverage of the United States.

3. In the *Propaedia* volume turn to part 6: *Art.* There is an introductory essay by Mark Van Doren. The listing begins with art in general, followed by the particular arts. Under both music and dance, see the subject outlines and suggested readings in the encyclopedia. Repeat this with a subject of choice, or the history of mankind, or, under matter and energy, division 1, the structure and properties of atoms. Note that at the end of the outlines there are cross-references to biographies and to the *Index*.

   At the back of the *Propaedia*, there is the notably long list of editors, advisers, contributors, and authorities.

4. Look up several of the subjects cited in the above examples in the two-volume *Index*, then locate them in the encyclopedia. You will find the *Index* entries listed by volume, page number, column, and placement in the column, separated by colons, as 2:462:3b. A guide

to the use of the *Index* and a key to abbreviations are provided in each of the two volumes.

5. The consensus of most reviewers is that the *New Britannica* is suitable for senior high school and college students as well as adults. It retains the traditional quality, depth, and authoritative coverage of its predecessors.

CHILDREN'S AND YOUNG ADULT SOURCES

AE
5
W55

THE WORLD BOOK ENCYCLOPEDIA
Chicago, World Book, 1988. 22v. il.

The *World Book* was first published in 1917, and, through its editorial and annual revision policies, has maintained an outstanding reputation. It is written primarily for elementary through high school students, but is also an informative work for adults.

Articles are based on continuing research in representative courses of study, from kindergarten through high school, at hundreds of schools. The articles are graded, written at the levels of the persons most likely to look up the subjects. Some of the articles, such as that on computers, begin with a simple explanation and build toward complex concepts and a higher reading level. The arrangement is alphabetical, word by word.

1. The preface gives a useful overview of the editorial philosophy and contents. Read the section "How to Use *World Book*." This is followed by a section on other research aids, a pronunciation key, and a list of contributors and consultants.

2. Examples of long, generously illustrated articles can be found in the entries for *airplane* and *animal*. (The contributors are identified in an inset at the end of the first column.)

   For the comprehensive coverage given to countries, look up Australia. The article includes a section of facts in brief, a colored illustration with an explanation of the flag, a political map with an index, and information on all aspects of the peoples of the country/continent—the history, government, culture, and economy. The section on land regions is illustrated with color maps of subjects such as terrain, climate, and locations of animals and plants. Notice the color quality of the photographs. The article ends with a list of related articles, questions, and two bibliographies—one for young readers and another for older readers.

3. For representative articles on science and technology, turn to physics and nuclear weapons. The article on the human body has transparent color overlays to clarify the location of parts of the body. For the coverage of forms of art, see the articles on stained glass and painting.

4. Choose one of the fifty states and refer to the entry. How much and what kind of information is provided? Notice the interesting facts and facts in brief sections; the depictions of state symbols and maps; and the study aids.

   The history and description of many of the world's large cities are given in detail, as for Atlanta and Toronto.

5. Volume 22 contains the comprehensive index to the set; an instructional section titled "A Student Guide to Better Writing, Speaking, and Research Skills"; and more than 200 reading and study guides.

Continue with your own comparative analysis of the *World Book Encyclopedia* with the *Merit Students Encyclopedia* (William D. Halsey, Editorial Director; Emanuel Friedman, Editor-in-Chief. N.Y., Macmillan Educational Co., 1988. 20v.). Refer to the introduction to this chapter for features to consider. Are the content, style, and format suitable for the intended readers? Is it well illustrated? Is there a comprehensive index? Select several subjects to determine currency of the information. Compare these with articles on the same subjects in the *World Book*.

SUBJECT ENCYCLOPEDIAS

General encyclopedias cannot feasibly present detailed studies of all subjects in depth, or give sophisticated, advanced coverage sufficient to satisfy specialists. Reference works published for specific fields are now frequently found in libraries other than college, university, and special libraries because of the increasing demand created by higher educational levels in the general adult population, and the ever-broadening interests of readers. For this reason, several subject encyclopedias were selected for inclusion in this work as examples. These barely reflect the numbers and kinds of encyclopedias in specialized fields.

Each specialty has its basic reference sources, such as directories, dictionaries, handbooks, indexes, abstracts, biographical dictionaries, and bibliographies, and there are specialties within specialties. As a reference librarian, you are expected to be aware of their availability and expert in the use of those in your collection. The six examples described here do not represent a departure from the purpose of this book because their content, authority, and style of presentation make them usable and valuable assets in a general reference collection.

Z
1006
A18

ALA WORLD ENCYCLOPEDIA OF LIBRARY AND INFORMATION SERVICES
Robert Wedgeworth, Editor
Chicago, American Library Association, 1986.
xxv, 895p. il.

The *ALA World Encyclopedia of Library and Information Services* provides international coverage of the history, functions, services, present status and future of libraries, librarians, information specialists, and others associated with the field.

The editor states that, in this revised edition, the "historical articles trace the development of the field, an overview enriched by current description of library and information services in countries around the world. Professional concepts and principles are explained and . . . biographies bring to life the major activities in the lives of persons who have played a part in shaping the field" (Preface). The encyclopedia was prepared with the assistance of 411 contributors (p. ix–xvii) and 31 advisers (p. iv).

An outline of contents is provided "as a guide to the organization of knowledge of the field" (Preface). It has five principal divisions: "The Library in Society," "The Library as an Institution," "Theory and Practice of Librarianship," "Education and Research," and "International Library, Information, and Bibliographic Organizations." Look carefully through the outline to understand the range, order, and detail of the coverage. There is a comprehensive index at the back of the book.

The signed articles are arranged alphabetically; many have brief bibliographies.

1. Read the article on at least one of the "major types of institutions." These are listed in part 2 of the outline of contents (p. xxiii). Note that the listing includes the organization of the articles.

2. For information on two of the current concerns of the profession, refer to the articles "Censorship" and "Certification." A background for the latter can be found under "Library education: History"; and "Librarianship, Profession of."

3. The subjects of biographies are included in part 1 of the outline of contents by period and place and under the individual's name in the index. Look up Margaret Mann, Robert B. Downs, and Robert G. Vosper. Remember that the representation is international and includes publishers and philanthropists who contributed to the field. The histories of national libraries are enlivened by the biographies of their directors, as *Herbert Putman, Library of Congress; Frank Bradway Rogers and Martin M. Cummings, National Library of Medicine;* and others who made notable contributions and are referred to in these sketches.

4. "Articles cover the status and condition of libraries in countries of the world and provide statistics" (Preface). As an example, turn to the article on Canada. A brief general history of Canadian libraries is given, followed by descriptions of types of libraries, statistics, "the profession," and the national library associations. There are photo-illustrations of uniquely modern libraries (p. 162–163).

5. To learn more about the special coverage of this encyclopedia, choose and read about a service or topic that interests you, as children's services, online information services, micrographics, archives, copyright, services to the handicapped, or international library organizations.

<table>
<tr><td>E
174
D52</td><td>**DICTIONARY OF AMERICAN HISTORY,
Revised ed.**
N.Y., Scribner, 1976. 8v.</td></tr>
</table>

The first edition of the *Dictionary of American History,* published in 1940, "was undertaken in response to the demands of historians and librarians for a reference work of American history in which exact information about the thousands of separate facts of American history that are so difficult to locate elsewhere could be found easily and quickly" (Foreword).

The articles, in alphabetical order by subject, are written by experts and scholars. Each is signed; many have brief bibliographies. The revised edition expanded the coverage on Native Americans, Afro-Americans, the arts, science, and technology. "The index of the revised edition of the *Dictionary* is not simply a listing of proper names, but a thorough analytical listing of every item of information in the *Dictionary* under all its possible headings" (Foreword).

1. The three entries on the first page of the first volume provide an excellent introduction to the subjects, the detail, and historical periods covered: See *Aachen; ABC Conference;* and *Abilene.*

2. This is a not-to-be-forgotten source on anything related to American history. Read some of the following entries: *Watergate; Whipple's Expedition; Webster-Hayne Debate; Bill of Rights; Traverse des Sioux Treaty.*

   There are long articles on *Labor; Taxation; Texas; Army, United States.*

   No biographies are included, but every person mentioned in the articles is listed in the index. (For biographies, reference is made to the *Dictionary of American Biography,* q.v.).

   The range of subjects on science, technology, and commerce can be seen in such entries as: space, veterinary medicine, borax, cereal grains and manufacture, and whaling; also see specific diseases that have had a large-scale impact on the population.

3. Volume 8 contains the comprehensive analytical index. It is important to read the introduction to the index for effective use. Note the errata list following the introduction and the list of abbreviations. For an appreciation of the detailed listings, turn to *Supreme Court.*

BL
31
E46

THE ENCYCLOPEDIA OF RELIGION
Mircea Eliade, Editor-in-Chief
N.Y., Macmillan, 1987. 16v. il.

"Such an encyclopedia as this has long been overdue. . . .In planning it, the editors and the staff have aimed at a concise, clear, and objective description of the totality of human experiences of the sacred. . . . [The encyclopedia] was conceived as a system of articles on important ideas, beliefs, rituals, myths, symbols, and persons that have played a role in the universal history of religions from Paleolithic times to the present day" (Preface).

The preface, foreword, and introduction present the concepts and aims considered in the preparation of the encyclopedia. The text is preceded by a listing of abbreviations and symbols.

1. Turn to the article on Afro-American religions. It begins with a brief summary of the coverage and *see* references to related articles, followed by an overview, from the legacy from Africa through the 1970s, with bibliography; the second part of the article concerns Muslim movements, with a bibliography and *see also* references to biographies of leaders of the movement.

2. The diversity of the subjects can be realized in looking up anti-Semitism, atheism, artificial intelligence, Australian religions, and touching. There is a long article, with drawings, on temples.

3. Biographies are of mythological figures and of people from ancient to contemporary times. The index should be referred to in looking up any subject, as there are multiple entries for notable biographees, as Martin Luther; Martin Buber; Martin Luther King, Jr.; and Thomas Merton. Many of the articles include annotated bibliographies.

4. Remember that subjects are presented in reference to the study of religion, not with various considerations, as on suicide and tobacco.

5. The index volume, 16, includes a directory of contributors and an alphabetical list of entries, with the name(s) of contributors, a synoptic outline of contents, and a comprehensive index with cross-references.

Look carefully through the *synoptic outline*, which makes possible the fullest use of the encyclopedia.

E
184
A1H35

**HARVARD ENCYCLOPEDIA OF
AMERICAN ETHNIC GROUPS**
Stephan Thernstrom, Editor; Ann Orlov, Managing Editor; Oscar Handlin, Consulting Editor
Cambridge, Mass., Belknap Press of Harvard University Press, 1980. xxv, 1,076p.

This comprehensive study of the peoples of the United States is a unique and valued reference work. There are articles on 106 ethnic groups, with 29 thematic essays, 87 maps, and other supplementary material, to provide an understanding of our heritage and contemporary citizenry. "The group entries . . . reveal the powerful cohesive forces that have made the United States a nation of nations, that restore luster to the motto on the seal of the United States: *E Pluribus Unum*. In 1782 when the motto was adopted it referred to the union forged from the thirteen separate colonies; subsequently it has come to suggest the ties that bind the remarkable array of diverse peoples who have settled here" (p. vii).

1. The introduction is very interesting and informative. Read particularly the list of features, on page vi, that characterize the groups selected for inclusion in the encyclopedia. On page viii, scan the checklist/outline for group entries that was given to each contributor as a preparation guide for the article on the assigned group. There is an impressive list of contributors and consultants.

2. The table of contents lists the name of the contributor after the title of each entry. Notice the subjects of the thematic essays and the lists of maps and tables.

   The ethnic groups and the subjects of the thematic essays are listed in a single alphabetical order. There are many cross-references.

3. "The Encyclopedia's underlying premise is that ethnicity, whether good or bad, has been and remains important in the American social fabric. The content . . . helps provide a sound basis for thinking through the complex value issues at stake in this emotionally and politically charged area" (p. iv). Read or at least look carefully through some of the thematic essays, as *American identity and Americanization; language; labor;* and *prejudice and discrimination, policy against.*

4. Turn to the article on the American Indians, which is divided by regions and by Indian groups within the regions. There are maps of the locations of Indian tribes on pages 60–61. Each regional coverage has an annotated bibliography. Read the article about Afro-Americans, which describes the "largest ethnic group in America" from its African origins to the American frontier, including information on slavery and racism, emancipation, and postemancipation, to the Freedom Now Movement and black achievement.

5. There are articles on religious groups, such as the Mormons and the Amish, and on groups "made in America" that "are not the same in character as immigrant or racial groups, but possess a historical identity of their own," such as the Appalachians and southerners. This reminds us of the editors' statement that 'to equate 'ethnic' with 'foreign' is a mistake" (p. vi).

6. Select an ethnic group that interests you to become familiar with the arrangement and scope of the material. The choices include the Norwegians, Mexicans, Koreans, Italians, Gypsies, Irish, Austrians, Poles, Greeks, and more; the cultural substance of the nation. The discussions begin with the dates of first migration to the New World then provide the background of the people, the "image of America," the establishment of communities (settlements), religion, education, politics, social and fraternal organizations, and achievements. An annotated bibliography follows.

7. There are two appendixes: an explanation of the methods of estimating the size of groups, and a representative statistical analysis from the U.S. Bureau of the Census.

Q
121
M3

McGRAW-HILL ENCYCLOPEDIA OF SCIENCE AND TECHNOLOGY, 6th ed.
N.Y., McGraw-Hill, 1987. 20v. il.

In the preface, the editor states that the *McGraw-Hill Encyclopedia of Science and Technology* is "a work *of*, not *about* science. . . . This edition of the Encyclopedia explores all important developments and achievements since 1982."

At the beginning of volume 1, you will find the listing of the advisory board, the editorial staff, and consulting editors. Read the preface and the section on the organization of the encyclopedia.

Each entry is written by an expert in the particular field, "and the level of writing is consistent with the nature and degree of complexity of the subject, but all articles are written for the nonspecialist. The name of the author appears at the end of each article" (Preface).

The text for survey articles begins with a definition of the subject and background material, proceeding to more detailed and complex coverage. There are many cross-references (set in small capitals), which refer the reader to specific, related topics. The alphabetical arrangement of article titles is word by word.

1. The variety of subjects presented range from ecology to fiber optics, computers to diseases, genetic engineering to agricultural products. As examples of coverage in long articles, see *food engineering, integrated circuits*, and *Antarctic Ocean/Antarctica*.

   Technology is further represented by such subjects as *electric power systems* and *jig, fixture and die design*. You might consider the article on *free energy* an example of complex, advanced science material!

   Some bibliographies, including those for subjects undergoing steady, current research, development, and change, are outdated, or include chiefly works for background material, as the bibliographies for the articles on *air traffic control, aircraft propulsion*, and *acoustooptics*.

2. Volume 20 contains the list of contributors; information on scientific notation (don't overlook the section on making conversions between the international system, U.S. customary, and metric measurements); and the comprehensive *Analytical Index* and the *Topical Index*. Both indexes are preceded by an explanatory guide.

   Scan the *Topical Index*. This may well be an excellent starting point for future research on related subjects in a scientific field included in the encyclopedia.

ML
100
N48

THE NEW GROVE DICTIONARY OF MUSIC AND MUSICIANS
Edited by Stanley Sadie
London, Macmillan; Washington, D.C.,
Groves Dictionaries of Music, 1980. 20v. il.

In the preface of this famous, respected work the editor states, "The world—certainly the world of musicology—has changed more, and more fundamentally, in the twenty-five years that separate *Grove 5* from the new dictionary than it did in the 75 years from 1879 (when the first complete volume of the first edition appeared) to 1954. A very much smaller portion of material—under three per cent—has been retained from earlier editions than was retained in any preceding edition." Although it is titled a dictionary, the work is encyclopedic, both in number of volumes and in detail and scope of coverage.

Every subject that relates to music is considered: forms, histories, periods, schools, composers, musicians, performers, musical instruments, music of nations and peoples, cities and their musical heritage, and ideas and people that have influenced or contributed to music, with illustrations and bibliographies. However, "the dictionary's first task, traditionally, is to treat of the people who have written music; more than half the entries are on composers, from ancient and even mythological times to the present. . . . Other persons entered in the dictionary fall into five broad categories . . ." (Preface). Those categories are: (1) performers from the past and present; (2) scholars, writers, theorists, and administrators; (3) people in other arts whose work is important to music, such as librettists, authors, dancers, and designers; (4) patrons; and (5) people concerned with the business of music, from publishing to the making of musical instruments.

Read the introduction, which provides instructions on the use of the work. It is followed by the preface to the first edition, written by Sir George Grove, which presents the enduring philosophy and intent of the dictionary.

1. After the introduction and preface, you will find the listings of general abbreviations, bibliographical abbreviations, and library sigla. To be certain that you understand this last list, turn to page 1 (50). In the second column, you will see: *US: United States of America.* The libraries are listed in alphabetical order by place. Scan through to *NY.* If you were looking for the Juilliard School of Music, you would find it cited after *NYj.*

2. With volume 1 still in hand, turn to the article on *acoustics.* It begins with the meanings of the word, with cross-references to related articles. The article extends from page 43 to page 86, covering the subject with references to sound-source acoustics (rooms), instruments, and the voice. Note the many graphs and the drawings of theaters, churches, and stages. There is a bibliography for each section.

3. The scholarship and detail presented in the biographies can be verified in the article on Beethoven, which is approximately sixty pages long. The last section lists his compositions and a bibliography divided into biographical titles and studies of his works.

4. There is an interesting entry on the national anthems of the world, found under *national.* Brief details are given about each, with the score for the opening lines.

5. To appreciate the scope of the articles, look up a comprehensive subject such as opera, notations, troubadours, or the history of a

musical instrument, such as the violin, organ, oboe, or guitar. If you look for an entry for rock music, you are referred to *popular music*.

The varied coverage is further demonstrated in the biographies of (Leon) Bix Beiderbecke, jazz musician great of the 1920s, and Irving Berlin; and an article on blues.

6. There are biographies of internationally known conductors, such as Arturo Toscanini, Leonard Bernstein, and Carlo Maria Giulini. Each has a bibliography and photo portrait.

7. As an example of the articles on the music of countries, turn to the article on Greece. Following a comprehensive history of music in Greece from ancient to contemporary times, there is a section, beginning on page 675, on folk music. Notice the excerpts from scores that illustrate explanations in the text. The article includes a section on folk music of Greek emigrant communities.

8. At the end of volume 20, appendix A is an index of terms used in articles on non-Western music, folk music, and kindred topics. The set ends with appendix B, a list of contributors.

ENCYCLOPEDIAS

Additional Titles

Childcraft—The How and Why Library. Chicago, World Book, 1985. 15v.

Children's Britannica. Chicago, Encyclopaedia Britannica, 1988. 20v.

Compton's Encyclopedia. Chicago, Encyclopaedia Britannica, 1988. 26v.

Encyclopedia of the Third World, 3d ed. By George Thomas Kurian. N.Y., Facts on File, 1987. 3v.

Encyclopedia of World Art. N.Y., McGraw-Hill, 1968, 1983. 16v. (v. 16 supplement.)

The Facts on File Encyclopedia of World Mythology and Legend. By Anthony S. Mercante. N.Y., Facts on File, 1988.

McGraw-Hill Encyclopedia of World Drama: An International Reference Work, 2d ed. Stanley Hochman, Editor-in-Chief. N.Y., McGraw-Hill, 1984. 5v.

The New Book of Knowledge. Danbury, Conn., Grolier, 1988. 21v.

Worldmark Encyclopedia of the Nations. N.Y., Worldmark Press, 1988. 5v.

Worldmark Encyclopedia of the States, 2d ed. N.Y., Worldmark Press, 1986.

3.

YEARBOOKS, ANNUALS, AND ALMANACS

The goal of a reference librarian is to be able to turn to a known source to find appropriate and authoritative answers to patrons' inquiries. Whether called on to help a researcher ferret out the oldest recorded statistics on a South American Indian tribe or to give a high school student the latest count of membership of the United Nations, the librarian should know where to look for the answer, or for a source or service that might provide the answer.

A reliable almanac supplies facts, figures, and summaries of trends and recent events in a succinct, clear, and simple style. Some almanacs are worldwide in scope, whereas others confine themselves to a particular locality. Each has a place and function in the reference collection.

Encyclopedia yearbooks serve not only to update specific subjects treated within the already published encyclopedia, but also to review and describe national and international events of the preceding year in far more detail than is possible in the normal revision of the encyclopedia. Because of this detailed treatment of major events for a given year, the value of encyclopedia yearbooks is enhanced with the passage of time. A cumulative index in the latest volume is helpful in locating an article on a particular topic for a specific year.

Specialized annual or biennial publications should not be overlooked. These vary with the nature of the organization responsible for their publication and increase the scope of the reference collection. The librarian's task is to become so familiar with the best of the many available sources that their appropriate use to meet a need becomes a conditioned reflex. It is essential to keep abreast of new publications, features, and topics, and of changes in the arrangement of new editions of continuing publications.

The present chapter introduces a number of standard annuals, almanacs, and yearbooks. As you study each volume, pose questions to see if the volume provides a satisfactory answer. Look for the answers in several sources mentioned in this chapter, and compare the information, ease of locating it, and style in which it is presented. Continued practice results in mastery of these basic tools.

Z
1033
P3A58

THE BOWKER ANNUAL OF LIBRARY AND BOOK TRADE INFORMATION

N.Y., R. R. Bowker, 1956–   . Annual.

The *Bowker Annual* is a practical compendium covering a broad range of news, facts, statistics, and activities concerning libraries, librarianship, the information industry, and the book industry. It provides information on professional organizations; statistics on book production and distribution; legislation affecting libraries and publishing; salaries of library personnel; updates on publishers' mergers; and lists of notable books and library prizes.

1. In the 1988–89 edition, look up high technology bibliography, scholarships, guide to library placement sources, the calendar, and the chart of new public library buildings.

G
122
C67

COUNTRIES OF THE WORLD AND THEIR LEADERS/YEARBOOK

Detroit, Gale Research, 1974–   . il., maps.

"Countries of the World and Their Leaders/Yearbook is intended as a one-step reference source to answer the everyday questions arising about the world's countries. It takes a synoptic look at every one of the world's nations outside the United States to provide the general overview of the individual country that would be important to the student, the businessperson, or the traveler. ... The two primary sources for the data herein are the U.S. Department of State ... and the Central Intelligence Agency" (Introduction, p. xi). Much of the data presented is based on *Background Notes*, the series of country profiles issued by the State Department.

The 1988 *Yearbook* is in two volumes. The introduction to volume 1 outlines the eleven sections contained in the work.

1. The first section in volume 1 is the alphabetic listing of chiefs of state and cabinet members of foreign countries, followed by an alphabetic name index. The second section, "Status of the World's Nations," begins with an interesting survey of the formation and recognition of nations; that leads to the list of nations, dependencies, and areas of Special Sovereignty. This provides "capsules of key facts" on each country. Newly independent countries (since 1943) are shown in alphabetical and chronological checklists. The third section of volume 1 is a directory of key officers and addresses

of U.S. embassies, consulates, and foreign service posts, in alphabetical order by country. There is an outline on how and where to seek the State Department's assistance when doing business abroad, a list of abbreviations and symbols, and instructions on accepted forms for addressing mail to a foreign service post.

2. The *Background Notes on Countries of the World,* which form the main text, are in alphabetical order. For each country there is a map, the short and the official name of the country, and a profile with facts and statistics on people, geography, government, economy, and membership in international organizations. These categories are then repeated in articles giving more detailed information, including history, government and political conditions, foreign relations, travel notes, a bibliography, and the names and addresses of principal U.S. officials stationed in the country.

3. Select and review the coverage of one of the world's major countries and one of the newly independent countries, as Belize or Burkina Faso. As examples of the coverage given nations recently receiving world media attention, see the articles on the political conditions and foreign relations of the Union of South Africa and of Libya.

   There is no index for the *Background Notes,* but there is one for the preceding listing of chiefs of state and cabinet members. The political rise of Mikhail Gorbachev is described in the text on the Soviet Union, but he is not in the index. Colonel Mu'ammar al'Qadhafi of Libya is described as having no official title, but is included in the index.

4. The section on foreign travel is a comprehensive compilation of information on health, customs, regulations, passports, visas, government advice, travel warnings, and advisories. There is an extraordinary provision of health information for international travel based on a report by the U.S. Centers for Disease Control, which includes vaccination requirements, U.S. Public Health Service Recommendations, potential health hazards, transportation of pets, etc., ending with indexes by subject and country.

5. The articles on international treaty organizations include the United Nations, NATO, the Organization of African Unity, and others, giving background, structure, membership, accomplishments and a bibliography.

6. The final section is on climates of the world. Charts indicate the latitude, longitude, elevations, average year-round temperatures and precipitation for "more than 550 key cities of the world" by continent, country, and city.

7. In each year since 1981, excepting 1984, a midyear *Countries of the World/Yearbook Supplement* has been published to provide updated reports issued by the Department of State.

JA
51
S7

STATESMAN'S YEAR-BOOK:
Statistical and Historical Annual
of the States of the World, 1864–   .
London, Macmillan, 1864–   ; New York,
St. Martin's Press. Annual.

The *Statesman's Year-book*, which gives a concise description and statistical facts about every country in the world, has proved to be an accurate and reliable source of information for reference librarians. John Paxton has been the editor since 1970.

1. Examine the table of contents. Following statistical tables and addenda, the book is divided into two major sections: "International Organizations" and "Countries of the World."

2. The detailed index, with its many *see* references, provides the quickest and surest way to locate information stored in this useful volume.

3. Look up Quebec, Canada. Note the details given, which include a brief history, area and population, climate, constitution and government, religion, economy, and education.

4. Look through the lengthy, detailed section on the United States.

5. Does the Netherlands have compulsory military service? Does its army participate as a part of the NATO forces?

6. Where are the headquarters of the International Narcotics Control Board, and what are its functions?

HA
202
A5

**STATISTICAL ABSTRACT OF THE
UNITED STATES, 1878–**
U.S. Bureau of the Census
Washington, D.C., U.S. Government
Printing Office, 1879– . Annual.

"The Statistical Abstract of the United States, published since 1878,
is the standard summary of statistics on the social, political, and
economic organization of the United States. . . .

"This volume includes a selection of data from many statistical
publications, both government and private. . . . Except as indicated,
figures are for the United States as presently constituted. Although
emphasis in the *Statistical Abstract* is given primarily to national
data, many tables present data for regions and individual states and
a smaller number for metropolitan areas and cities" (Preface). The
source for the printed data of each table is clearly indicated.

Librarians should be familiar with the various supplements to the
Statistical Abstract. They are available from the Superintendent of
Documents and are priced so that even low-budget libraries can afford
them.

1. Read the preface and guide to tabular presentation. Look carefully
   through the table of contents. Here you are introduced to the broad
   fields that are covered statistically.

2. Each section has an introductory article that explains the coverage
   and sources of data for the tables that follow. As examples, read
   the interesting introductions to the sections on law enforcement,
   courts and prisons; and national defense and veterans affairs.

3. Turn to the table "City Governments—Finances, Largest Cities."
   Compare the revenue and expenditures of the four most populous
   cities. What are the differences in their expenditures for health
   and hospitals, police and fire protection? Do you find expenditures
   for the support of public libraries listed? Were you surprised at the
   rank in population of Houston, Texas?

4. You will find statistics on seemingly limitless categories—im-
   munization of children, marriage, environment, hazardous waste
   sites, taxes, employment, climate, elections, and immigration.
   And this is only a small sample!
       The last section of the main text contains comparative inter-
   national statistics.

5. There are five appendixes, including a guide to sources of statistics and to statistical methodology and reliability.
   Be certain to examine carefully the comprehensive index at the end of the book.

Supplementary publications include: U.S. Bureau of the Census. *County and City Data Book*, 1949– . Washington, D.C., U.S. Government Printing Office, 1952– .
―――. *Historical Statistics of the United States, Colonial Times to 1970.* Washington, D.C., U.S. Government Printing Office, 1975. 2v.

JK
421
A3

**UNITED STATES GOVERNMENT
MANUAL, 1935–**
Washington, D.C., 1935– . Annual. Publisher varies:
Office of the Federal Register National Archives and
Records Administration. Available from
Superintendent of Documents, U.S. Government
Printing Office, Washington, D.C., 20402

"As the official handbook of the Federal Government, *The United States Government Manual* provides comprehensive information on the agencies of the legislative, judicial, and executive branches. The *Manual* also includes information on quasi-official agencies, international organizations in which the United States participates, boards, committees, and commissions.
A typical agency description includes a list of principal officials, a summary statement of the agency's purpose and role in the Federal Government, a brief history of the agency, including its legislative or executive authority, a description of its programs and activities, and a 'Sources of Information' section" (Preface).

1. Proceed slowly in your examination of this important annual. Look at the table of contents first to get the overall outline of the government's organization.

2. The *Manual* opens with a copy of the *Declaration of Independence* and the *Constitution of the United States*, including all the amendments to date. If a patron asks for a copy of the *Bill of Rights*, do you know where to find it?

3. The first branch of government described is the legislative branch. The names of the officers/leaders, the standing committees, ses-

sions, powers, publications, and rosters of the senators and representatives are given. Among the offices and agencies under this branch, note that the Library of Congress is included.

4. In the section on the judicial branch, the members of the Supreme Court, the terms and jurisdiction are listed, followed by the organization, rosters and authority of the lower courts, the U.S. Courts of Appeal, and district and special courts.

5. Look through the detailed data on the executive branch, which includes the staffs and organization of the departments. What agencies are under the Department of the Treasury? When was the Bureau of Alcohol, Tobacco and Firearms established? What are its responsibilities?

6. As an example of the information given for other agencies, look up the location of the field installations of the National Aeronautics and Space Administration.

7. At the end of each entry, sources are cited for additional information.

The five appendixes include the standard federal regions; terminated, transferred, or changed-in-name agencies; agencies appearing in the Code of Federal Regulations; and commonly used abbreviations.

The indexes are by name and agency/subject.

8. At the end of the *Manual,* there is an addendum for recent changes and pending actions relating to personnel included in the text.

QC   **THE WEATHER ALMANAC . . . , 5th ed.**
983   **Edited by James A. Ruffner and Frank E. Bair**
R83   Detroit, Gale Research, 1987. viii, 811p. il., maps

The editors state in the introduction that the *"Weather Almanac* provides a wide range of maps, charts, and safety rules based upon past records and experience to inform you (as far as possible in a single volume) of what may be expected from the restless atmosphere. . . . *Weather Almanac* offers you a great storehouse of data from hundreds of sources, assembled and presented in forms to let you look up detailed facts as you need them. . . . Much of the information in this book is quoted directly from reports and records prepared by various United States Government departments, agencies, and services which share parts of the nation's great weather and environmental science efforts." Most of the coverage is on the United States, but there is a section, "Round-the-World Weather," which lists temperatures and precipitation data for 550 cities around the world.

Look carefully through the table of contents, which provides a detailed outline of the data presented.

1. The first section, "U.S. Weather in Atlas Format," is a collection of maps on which temperature, precipitation, snowfall, frost, sunshine, and wind data for various key points in the United States are presented in charts by month. Note the legends in the lower right corners of the odd-numbered pages, and the insets for Alaska and Hawaii.

   The second section is on storms, severe weather, and geophysical phenomena. The causes and results, and the survival safety rules for major occurrences of hurricanes, tornadoes, floods, earthquakes, etc., are described and charted. See the special features that follow, such as those on air pollution and weather fundamentals, a glossary of weather terms, and record-setting weather to round-the-world weather.

2. The round-the-world weather charts are by continent, country, or region and city ("station"). Look up Copenhagen, Denmark. You will find the latitude, longitude, elevation, the number of years of records represented, and the temperature and precipitation averages and extremes.

3. The section "Weather of 109 Selected U.S. Cities" begins with instructions in "How to Read These Reports." After studying the explanations, choose a city and learn what data is given. There is a brief introduction for each city and an inset of reference notes to define the symbols and terms.

   For Minneapolis, Minnesota, in table 1, under precipitation, what does "water equivalent" mean? In table 6, under snowfall for October 1957–58, what does "T" indicate?

   Compare the record highest and lowest temperatures for Los Angeles and Honolulu.

4. The librarian may need to advise the reader that the charts and tables cite locations where official records were taken, which are described in the accompanying text; as the location of the highest temperature officially recorded in the United States is listed on a

Record-Setting Weather chart as Greenland Ranch, California. The accompanying text describes the ranch, located in Death Valley.

5. The world maps and photo illustrations could be improved. Some errors were found in the index, for the paging of jet-lag, and Weather Radio. There is no entry for the National Oceanic and Atmospheric Administration (NOAA), which provides the service Weather Radio, described with a table of the network on pages 282–83. However, the comprehensive, detailed data is presented in an understandable, clear form in the text, tables, and charts, and supplies immediate ready reference answers to a wide variety of questions, from the complex, "What is atmospheric ozone?" to the simpler, "What is the difference between weather and climate?"

AY	**THE WORLD ALMANAC AND**
67	**BOOK OF FACTS, 1868–**
N5W7	N.Y., Newspaper Enterprise Association,
	Pharos Books. Annual.

The *World Almanac* has long been a favorite of reference librarians. The first edition was published in 1868, and, except for a ten-year suspension from 1876 to 1886, this extraordinary compilation of miscellaneous information has been published annually.

1. The comprehensive index is at the beginning of the book. At the end of the index, there is a section for addenda, late news, changes, and corrections. On the last page of the *Almanac*, there is a quick reference index that may save time for general categories.

2. Even experienced librarians are sometimes surprised at the variety of information the *Almanac* provides. Use the index to find the answers to the following questions:
   a. What states do not observe daylight saving time?
   b. Where were the 1988 Winter Olympic games held?
   c. How many electoral votes does Idaho have?
   d. What is the capital of West Virginia?
   e. Who is the head of state of Belgium?

3. Do you know that you can find the following in *The World Almanac?*
   a. A biographical summary for each U.S. president;

b. the *Declaration of Independence* and the *Constitution of the United States* and the amendments;
c. the sizes (heights, lengths, and depths) of world mountains, rivers, and lakes;
d. a labor union directory;
e. statistics on U.S. population, economy, etc.;
f. the winners of national and international awards and prizes;
g. the number of members of the U.S. armed forces who served in Vietnam;
h. the names, terms, and salaries of state governors.

Compare this almanac with one cited in the list of additional titles at the end of this chapter.

AE
5
W55

**THE WORLD BOOK YEAR BOOK:
The Annual Supplement to
the World Book Encyclopedia**
Chicago, World Book, [1962]–   . il. Annual.

As a supplement to the *World Book Encyclopedia*, the *Year Book* provides a chronology and description of events of the year preceding the year of publication. There are articles of current special interest; revised articles reprinted from the encyclopedia; and a dictionary supplement, which lists "important words and definitions" from the latest edition of the *World Book Dictionary* (q.v.).

1. Look over the contents pages to see what is included and how the volume is arranged. See the month-by-month calendar of events; special reports; a review of happenings in the year in the previous century (the 1988 *Year Book*, listing events for 1987, would describe the year 1887). The section "Year on File" includes signed articles, in alphabetical order, on major developments of the year. In the 1988 *Year Book*, note the coverage of the Iran-Contra affair; the Congress of the United States; civil rights; weather; literature and literature for children; and the tabulated data on sports, governments, and nations. There are brief biographies of persons who received national or international attention, such as given, in 1987, to Oliver L. North, William S. Sessions, and Robert J. Dole.

   For articles throughout the *Year Book*, *see* references are given to related articles in the encyclopedia. The volumes are generously illustrated.

The cumulative index covers the contents of the current and two preceding editions of the *Year Book.*

Continue with your own comparative analysis. Compare *Compton's Yearbook* with the *World Book Year Book,* and compare the *Britannica Book of the Year* with the *Americana Annual* or *Collier's Year Book.*

1. The publishers of encyclopedias present their yearbooks as supplements that update the information in the encyclopedias. However, some of the yearbooks provide only an overview, including a chronology, with brief commentary, on the major national and international events of the preceding year and other special features that do not have a real relationship to the articles in the encyclopedias.

    Do the yearbooks you are comparing relate to the encyclopedias in arrangement, subject headings, and articles? Do the articles in the yearbook update the information found in the encyclopedias? How are the chronology of the year's events, illustrations, statistics, and factual data combined with the other parts of the work? Is the content and style of the yearbook appropriate for the intended users of the encyclopedia? Is there a comprehensive index?

JX
1977
A37Y4

YEARBOOK OF THE UNITED NATIONS, 1946/47–
N.Y., United Nations, Department of
Public Information, 1947–   .

The United Nations *Yearbook* "has been designed as a reference tool for use not only by diplomats and other officials but also by writers, researchers, journalists, librarians and students, in fact all who might need readily available information on a particular activity of the United Nations system" (1984 *Yearbook,* p. xiii). In this work, the debates, decisions, resolutions, reports and activities of the UN and the related specialized international agencies are chronicled to form an important component of the UN's historical record.

1. Look carefully at the detailed table of contents. Part 1 is divided into five major sections, covering political and security issues, economic and social issues, trusteeship and decolonization, legal questions, and administrative and budgetary questions. Part 2 deals with related organizations in the UN system, such as

UNESCO and WHO. The acronyms are spelled out in the table of contents.

Read the introductory explanation of the text and see the list of abbreviations that follows.

2. Select one of the issues considered by the United Nations, such as treaties and agreements, food, the Middle East, and human rights, to learn the scope of information available in the *Yearbook*.

    Select also one of the special agencies, as the International Atomic Energy Agency or the World Meteorological Organization, for clarification of their functions.

    As an example of the text of a resolution, turn to page 959 in the 1984 *Yearbook*, the section "Economic and Social Questions: Drugs of Abuse," for General Assembly resolution 39/142.

3. The appendixes are important reference sources as they include the charter, members, and structure of the United Nations, and a directory of international information centers and services.

    There is a subject index, name index, and index of resolutions and decisions.

YEARBOOKS, ANNUALS, AND ALMANACS
Additional Titles

Almanac of American Politics. Washington, D.C., Barone, 1972– .
   Biennial. Publisher varies.
*American Book-Prices Current: A Record of Literary Properties Sold
   at Auction in England, the United States, and in Canada . . . 1894/
   1895– . N.Y., American Book-Prices Current, 1895– . Annual.
   Publisher varies.
*Chase's Annual Events. An Almanac and Survey of the Year: A Cal-
   endar of Holidays, Holy Days, National and Ethnic Days . . . the
   World Over.* Chicago, Contemporary Books, 1958– . Annual.
Educational Media and Technology Yearbook. Edited by Donald P. Ely.
   Englewood, Colo., Libraries Unlimited, 1973– .
Europa Year Book. London, Europa Publications, 1959– .
Guinness Book of World Records. N.Y., Sterling, 1956– . Annual.
*Information Please Almanac, Atlas and Yearbook, 1947– . Boston,
   Houghton Mifflin. Publisher varies.
Political Handbook of the World. N.Y., McGraw-Hill, 1975– . An-
   nual.

Whitaker's Almanack. London, Whitaker, 1869–   . Annual. U.S. distribution by Gale Research.

Writer's Market. Cincinnati, Ohio, Writer's Digest Books, 1928–   . Annual.

4.

HANDBOOKS AND MANUALS

In *Webster's Third,* a handbook is defined as "a concise reference book covering a particular subject or field of knowledge." Although *manual* is listed as a synonym for *handbook,* a distinction should be noted. Generally, a manual is a guide for performing a certain task, such as an automobile repair manual, or a manual of rules and procedures. A handbook helps one learn about specific aspects of a subject, such as a handbook of chemistry. The fact that the terms are sometimes used interchangeably may cause some confusion but no real problem. Books may be placed arbitrarily in one group or another if titles are clearly identified and presented within an explained purpose and plan. For the use of any reference source, you are advised to use the contents pages and/or the index. Whether a work is called a handbook, manual, almanac, or annual, the important object is to recognize the value of the tool and to develop skill in its use.

It must be kept in mind that the books discussed and cited in this chapter, as in all the chapters, are *examples* of types of reference books and do not represent a complete list.

GT
3930
G74

ANNIVERSARIES AND HOLIDAYS, 4th ed.
By Ruth W. Gregory
Chicago, American Library Association, 1983.
xiii, 262p.

"The purpose of *Anniversaries and Holidays* is to provide a quick identification of notable anniversaries, holy days, holidays, and special events days, and to link outstanding days to books for further information or background reading" (Preface). The scope is international, including dates, events and persons throughout history.

The text is divided into three parts: Part 1 is a calendar of fixed days by the months of the Gregorian calendar, with holy days and feast days, holidays and civic days, and anniversaries and special events days; part 2 contains calendars of movable days and includes the Christian Church, Islamic and Jewish calendars, and a calendar of movable feasts, festivals, and special events; part 3 is an annotated bibliography of books and other materials related to anniversaries and holidays for all age groups, with the exception of picture books having little text (p. viii). The three sections are followed by an index, which lists entries by date for part 1 and by page number for parts 2 and 3.

Read the preface, which describes the content and format, and the introduction, which provides an explanation of the history and types of calendars and a background on holidays in history.

1. In part 1, turn to the month of April. For each month, the original name and/or definition of the name is given, with the traditional observances and the flower(s) and gem(s) of the month.

   On April 1, under anniversaries and special events, the birthday of Sergei Rachmaninoff is listed. The number at the end of the entry refers to the numbered citation in the bibliography (part 3). Under April 16, you will find the "Feast of Saint Marie Bernarde Soubirous, popularly known as Saint Bernadette." The index has a cross-reference from the popular form to the religious name. For April 25, holidays and civic days, there is an entry for Anzac Day, with an explanation of the term *Anzac.*

2. Be aware of the detailed divisions of the bibliography in part 3.

3. In the entry for November 25, Thanksgiving day, a "c" is placed before the date. What does that indicate? Look up several of the multiple-numbered references in the bibliography.

PN
43
B65

BREWER'S DICTIONARY OF PHRASE AND FABLE, Centenary ed.
Revised by Ivor H. Evans
N.Y., Harper & Row, 1981. xvi, 1,213p.

"A reference book which has flourished for over a hundred years is clearly something exceptional. Its original compiler needs to hit upon not so much a new area of information of wide and permanent interest as a way of presenting that material and of providing access to it which satisfies and attracts generation after generation of readers" (p. vii). The first edition of *Brewer's* was published in 1870. *Brewer's* takes as its province the familiar and the unfamiliar in phrase, fable, romance, archaeology, history, religion, the arts, and the sciences.

Words that have no particular "tale to tell" and terms that can be found in standard dictionaries and encyclopedias are not included (p. v.). Entries have been updated, and the cross-referencing has been extended. There is an interesting biographical sketch of Dr. E. Cobham Brewer and a history of his dictionary in the introduction written by John Buchanan-Brown.

1. This book is fun to read as well as a useful reference aid. Every page offers intriguing and often unknown information. Here one finds such names and terms as *Alice, Psalms, Antigone, public-house signs, wedding finger,* and *lawyer's bags.* There is an article on libraries, including the largest libraries in the world. There are contemporary uses of terms, such as *Stonewall, the pill,* and *Big Brother.* Backgrounds are given for American terms and names, such as *blackboard jungle* and *Wells-Fargo.*

2. For examples of cross-referencing, look up *boogie-woogie;* you are referred to the added entries of *blues, ragtime,* and *swing.* If you look up *keeping up with the Joneses,* you will find the expression under *Jones,* followed by *"See under* KEEP."

3. There are helpful lists under *animals, assemblage,* and *rights.* Another "find" is the chart included for *watch,* which gives the times and names of the hours for a ship's crew to be on duty, "2000–2400 (8–12 midnight) First Watch."

Z
253
U69

THE CHICAGO MANUAL OF STYLE:
For Authors, Editors, and Copywriters,
13th ed.
Revised and expanded
Chicago, The University of Chicago Press, 1982.
ix, 738p.

As a reference librarian, you should be aware that this is much more than a guide to preparing manuscripts. It provides answers to many varied questions about writing. You will learn how much is included by looking at the table of contents listed at the beginning of each chapter.

The first published edition of the *Manual* was issued in 1906. The preface gives a brief background and statement of the philosophy of the original and present editors.

1. Paragraphs are numbered in consecutive order, and the index refers to those numbers rather than to page numbers.

2. Look through part 1, "Bookmaking: The Parts of a Book." There are definitions with illustrations of items that are basic for librarians but are sometimes overlooked. See paragraph 1.23 (p. 9). Did you know what CIP stands for? The Library of Congress Cataloging in Publication Data is a valuable help in many ways. There are several illustrations showing how well a book can be identified or described by referring to the CIP data on the copyright page, usually the verso of the title page.

3. The major emphasis is on detailed instruction for manuscript preparation and editing.

   Part 2, entitled "Style," is a ready-reference treasury of answers. The problems of punctuation and spelling are clarified. If you were asked whether the names of spacecraft, sculptures, or poems should be capitalized, quoted, or italicized (underscored), you would find examples in the chapter "Names and Terms." The index is comprehensive and lists each of these terms.

   Note the contents of chapter 9, "Foreign Language in Type" (p. 249). Chapter 12 has detailed advice on planning and constructing statistical tables. There are chapters on bibliographic forms and sections on the principles of alphabetizing, papermaking, and printing.

   At the end of the book there is a glossary of technical terms, bibliography, and index.

PN
6081
B27

FAMILIAR QUOTATIONS:
A Collection of Passages, Phrases, and
Proverbs Traced to Their Sources in
Ancient and Modern Literature,
15th and 125th anniversary ed.
Revised and enlarged by John Bartlett,
edited by Emily Morison Beck
Boston, Little, Brown, 1980. lviii, 1,540p.

Life is painting a picture,
not doing a sum.
——Oliver Wendell Holmes, Jr.,
The Class of '61. From
Speeches (1913)

This standard, popular work is traditionally referred to as "Bart-lett's." In the preface the editor advises us that "the first mission of a *Bartlett* editor is to assemble appropriate quotations from the years since the previous edition . . . [and] time will judge the validity of the fifteenth edition's choices from contemporary life and literature" (pp. vii–viii).

Read the preface and the historical note, which present a dynamic appreciation of the value and use of this work, first published in 1855. Study the brief section "Guide to the Use of *Familiar Quotations*." It is important to remember that in *Bartlett's*, "authors appear chronologically in birth date order. Under each author heading, quotations appear chronologically by date of publication" (p. xiv). There is an index of authors in the front of the book and an index to keywords of quotations at the end of the book.

1. Note the extensive entries from the Bible and Shakespeare, and the anonymous listings that immediately follow a quotation from the last dated author, Stevie Wonder. There are quotations with their sources dating from 2650 B.C. to the present.

2. Many of the quotations or excerpts encourage us to read the entire work. Have you filed Edith Wharton in the attic with the other classics? Read the selections included here on the chance that you will find a new interest.

   Turn to the humorous, serious, diverse quotations from the writings of E. B. White. One perhaps surprising quote is a famous cartoon caption. If you did not know the name of the author, could you find it through the keyword index? The index entries include the page number and the number of the quotation on the page.

3. In the listing of quotations from the works of William Butler Yeats, on page 712, the source of quotation no. 3 is given as *The Rose* (1893). *To the Rose upon the Rood of Time, st. 1;* the source of quotation no. 4 is *Ib. The Lake Isle of Innisfree, st. 1;* and of quotation no. 5, *Ib. st. 3.* Could you explain these and the following entries for Yeats to a student?

4. Some of the important features of *Bartlett's* include the very detailed index (pp. 939–1540) and the extensive cross-referencing of variants and backgrounds of quotations, pseudonyms, and original texts of translations.

AG
5
K315

FAMOUS FIRST FACTS: A Record of First Happenings, Discoveries, and Inventions in American History, 4th ed.
By Joseph Nathan Kane
Expanded and Revised
N.Y., H. W. Wilson, 1981. 1,350p.

"*Famous First Facts* now includes more than 9,000 firsts in American history. These pertain to Americans and to events that have occurred in the United States" (Preface).

The arrangement is alphabetical by subject, with generous cross-references. The four indexes are by year, day of the month, personal name, and geography. The variety and number of subjects are extraordinary.

1. Most of the general subjects are followed by specific subdivisions. Look at the entry for ships, then at the many subheadings. In addition to those, there are entries for specific types of ships. What is the name of the first aircraft carrier with an angle deck?

2. As additional examples of the range of subjects, you can find out about the first president's wife depicted on a commemorative postage stamp; the first baseball player to win the Most Valuable Player Award three times; the first ice cream sundae; and the first medical magazine.

   You might help a student who needs to know the name of an inventor and has not located it in a standard source by looking up the item invented as a "first."

3. The indexes by year and by day of the month provide not only a different way of gaining information about "firsts," but also a historical view of "progress."

   Think of a date—the day of a month—of an important past event, perhaps your birthday, and read the other "firsts" that occurred in preceding or successive years.

   The index of personal names lists the subjects and subheadings (if any) under which you may find the complete entry.

   The geographical index is alphabetical by state, and then city, with the subjects as they appear in the main body of the work.

4. Remember that all the "firsts" in this book apply to the United States only.

OCCUPATIONAL OUTLOOK HANDBOOK
Washington, D.C., Department of Labor,
Bureau of Labor Statistics, 1949–   .

"For nearly 40 years, the Bureau's *Occupational Outlook Handbook* has been a valuable source of career information" (Foreword). The *Handbook* is revised every two years.

1. Look through the table of contents. The occupations are listed in clusters of related occupations.

   The front of the book contains detailed guides to the use of the *Handbook* and to other sources of information. There are sections entitled "How to Get the Most from the Handbook," "Where to Go for More Information," and "Tomorrow's Jobs."

2. The pattern of the articles is the same for each occupation. Immediately below the heading, there are code numbers in parentheses. Turn to *librarians.* The code is: D.O.T. 100 except 100.167-010 and .367-018. "D.O.T." stands for *Dictionary of Occupational Titles* (U.S. Department of Labor, 4th ed. Washington, D.C., 1977; supplement, 1982). The codes are spelled out in the *Dictionary of Occupational Titles* index at the back of the *Handbook.* An explanation of these numbers is provided in an inset on page 1.

   The text on the occupations is subdivided into sections entitled "Nature of the Work," "Working Conditions," "Employment," "Training, Other Qualifications, and Advancement," "Job Outlook," "Earnings," "Related Occupations," and "Sources of Additional Information."

   Although most of the organizations listed for additional information are the primary professional associations, government offices, or national labor unions, users of the *Handbook* are advised that the Bureau of Labor Statistics does not investigate the organizations. "The listing of an organization, therefore, does not constitute in any way an endorsement or recommendation by the Bureau either of the organization and its activities or of the information it may supply" (note, p. iv).

3. Read the entries for several occupations in various categories to become familiar with the arrangement of information and the wide range of occupations.

4. Appendixes include summary data for occupations not covered in the handbook and sources of state and local job outlook information.

5. There is an alphabetically arranged index to occupations at the end of the volume.

PS
21
H3

THE OXFORD COMPANION TO
AMERICAN LITERATURE, 5th ed.
By James D. Hart
N.Y., Oxford University Press, 1983. 896p.

The *Companion* "provides ready references, first of all, to the authors and writings, past and present, popular and polite, that are included in the area of American literature . . . [and] . . . treats major nonliterary aspects of the American mind and the American scene as these are reflected in and influenced by American literature. . . . Foreign authors are also given attention . . . but the entries tell only of their American associations; and, of their works, only the ones that deal with America . . . are summarized in entries of their own" (Preface). Entries are in a single alphabetical arrangement.

1. The entries include brief biographies of authors, with bibliographies of their works, and contributors to American growth and culture; summaries of works (including poems, essays, and short stories); descriptions of songs, magazines, newspapers, religions, ethnic groups, cities, and geographic regions (as Plains). Characters of literary works are identified, with *see* references to the titles. There are cross-references for pseudonyms.

   As examples, see the entries for: Robert Penn Warren, James Thurber, Jessamyn West, Paul Horgan, Radcliffe College, Loop, "Patterns," and Little Giant.

2. A chronological index, pages 861–896, "is a year-by-year outline in parallel sequence of the social and literary history summarized in the *Oxford Companion to American Literature*" (p. 861).

The *Oxford Companions to English Literature and Children's Literature* are included in this chapter. There are also *Companions* to the literature of other countries that are helpful assets to a reference collection.

PR
19
H3

**THE OXFORD COMPANION TO
ENGLISH LITERATURE, 5th ed.**
Edited by Margaret Drabble
Oxford, Oxford University Press, 1985. xii, 1,155p.

The editor states in the preface that the purpose of this work remains the same as in the first edition (published in 1932), to be a "useful companion to ordinary everyday readers of English literature. . . . The emphasis has been on primary information rather than on critical appreciation. Works and authors are described and characterized rather than judged, although some attempt has been made to place them in context, and to account for shifts in reputation and taste."

The preface describes the choices and changes in this new edition.

1. The entries are in letter-by-letter alphabetical order. The "Note to the Reader," which immediately precedes the text, provides essential information on the entries.

2. For examples of articles on English authors, look up John Donne, William Makepeace Thackeray, Robert Graves, Harold Pinter, and Paul Scott.

   American authors are represented, including Nathaniel Hawthorne, Willa Cather, Marianne Moore, William Faulkner, and Richard Wright, as well as authors of all periods and other nations, as Plato and Epictetus to the modern Boris Pasternak and Gabriel Garcia Marquez.

   For other than established English authors, the provision of bibliographies is inconsistent.

3. Many and various subjects can be found in the *Companion*: fictional characters, summaries of works (including poems), terms, places, and movements. Read the entries for kitchen sink drama, magic realism, Friar Tuck, *What Maisie Knew, Little Dorrit*, "Eve of St. Agnes," Cambridge University Press, and *Manchester Guardian.*

   The work contains entries on composers as they relate to English literature. This is apparent in the article on Beethoven.

4. Several appendixes are provided at the end of the book: "Censorship and the Law of the Press," "Notes on the History of English Copyright," and "The Calendar."

CT
108
T83

**TWENTIETH CENTURY
AMERICAN NICKNAMES**
**Edited by Laurence Urdang;
compiled by Walter C. Kidney and George C. Kohn,
with a foreword by Leslie Alan Dunkling**
N.Y., H. W. Wilson, 1979. xi, 398p.

The entries include nicknames for persons, places, sports teams, crimes, initials, events, battles, military units, and organizations. In reference to the earlier work also published by H. W. Wilson, the editor "attempted to avoid duplication of nicknames appearing in George Earlie Shankle's *American Nicknames*. Also, the present work, unlike Shankle's, lists people, places and things that are sufficiently contemporary to admit of research in newspaper files, chronologies, and other sources that are easily accessible in libraries" (p. x). The sources for the information and the dates of first or chief usage are not given.

"All nicknames are listed in two places: alphabetically by the nickname itself and, in the same listing, alphabetically by surnames" (p. xi). The main entry includes birth and death dates or period of prominence, identification, and legal name if different from professional name. To be certain of the system of alphabetizing, see the entries under *Jack* and *Man*.

1. To check the method of cross-referencing, look up the nicknames *Stan the Man* and *Consumer Advocate*. If you knew that the champion boxer, Muhammad Ali, had a different name at birth, you would find it under the main entry, *Ali*. There is no other entry. However, there are separate entries for the multiple nicknames listed under *Harry Houdini*, *Atlanta, Georgia*, and *Theodore Roosevelt*.

2. Note the lists under *Murrow's Boys* and *Big Ten*. Nicknames of awards are identified, such as the *Obie*, *Tony*, and *Emmy*.

3. Some of the nicknames seem obscure or little used, such as those listed for *Doc* and *Colonel* and the *Outdoor Girl of the Films*. Other entries seem to stretch the possibility of use, such as the *Destroyer of the League of Nations* (Henry Cabot Lodge) and the *Renegade Newspaper Heiress* (Patricia Hearst).

4. Compare this work with Shankle's on the range of selections and data provided.

CHILDREN'S AND YOUNG ADULT SOURCES

PN
1008.5
C37

THE OXFORD COMPANION TO
CHILDREN'S LITERATURE
By Humphrey Carpenter and Mari Prichard
Oxford, Oxford University Press, 1984. xvi, 587p. il.

The editors state in the preface that the original plan for the *Oxford Companion to Children's Literature,* as proposed by Iona and Peter Opie, was to create "a reference book dealing equally with both English and American children's books and authors, and including articles on traditional materials, illustrators, characters from cartoons, films, radio and television, and the recurrent subjects of children's reading matter." The plan was followed within the limits of space demands made by the increase in the publication of children's books, and the addition of international coverage.

The preface gives the background of the work and the basis of selection of entries. Entries are in letter-by-letter alphabetical order.

1. There is a notable range of information in the *Companion.* There are histories of children's literature by country, as Australia, France, the United States, and Norway, and briefly by continent, as Africa and Latin America.

   Articles treat subjects represented in children's books and related interests, including racism, toy theater, adventure stories, Penny Dreadful, King Arthur, television, and moral tales.

2. Title entries vary from simple identification of the author or origin of a work to critical annotations, in addition to the entries for authors. Turn to *Little Women, Tailor of Gloucester, Wind in the Willows,* and *Winnie-the-Pooh.*

   Characters are identified by the title and author or origin of the works in which they appear.

   There are annotations for series, as *Earthsea* by Ursula Le Guin; for collections of poetry, as *When We Were Very Young* by A. A. Milne; for legends, as Robin Hood; and fairy stories, as Cinderella.

3. Motion pictures of special appeal to children are described. See *Fantasia* and *Snow White and the Seven Dwarfs.* There is a brief biography of Walt Disney and credits from Shirley Temple films adapted from children's classics. Note also the article on the television program *Sesame Street.*

Comics and animated cartoons are included. Little Orphan Annie, Bugs Bunny, and Mickey Mouse are examples. There is no entry for Charles Schulz, but under *Peanuts* and *Charlie Brown* you will find a *see* reference to *Snoopy*, where author credit and the beginning date of the comic strip are given.

4. The length of biographies varies from simple listings of the birth and death dates, nationality, and titles published, to an oddly brief coverage of E. B. White, to long articles, such as those on Lewis Carroll, Beatrix Potter, and Maurice Sendak.

5. Lists of the winners of the Newbery and Carnegie medals for children's authors are provided, but not for the Caldecott or the Kate Greenaway medals for illustrators.

HANDBOOKS AND MANUALS

Additional Titles

American Book of Days, 3d ed. Compiled and edited by Jane M. Hatch. N.Y., H. W. Wilson, 1978.
Benet's Reader's Encyclopedia, 3d ed. N.Y., Harper & Row, 1987.
Name of late, original editor, William Rose Benet, retained in title to acknowledge his contribution; a ready-reference treasury of brief articles, on not only world literature—authors, titles, characters, plots, etc.—but also on the varied interests of readers.
Book of the States. Lexington, Kentucky. Council of State Governments, 1935– . Biennial.
Congress and the Nation: A Review of Government and Politics, 1945–1964– . Washington, D.C., Congressional Quarterly Service, 1965– . Quadrennial.
Critical Survey of Poetry: English Language Series. Edited by Frank N. Magill. Englewood Cliffs, N.J., Salem Press, 1982. 8v.
Critical essays on poets and poetry, from *Beowulf* to present, with brief bibliographies. Indexes.
Dictionary of American Children's Fiction, 1859–1959: Books of Recognized Merit. By Alethea K. Helbig and Agnes Regan Perkins. Westport, Conn., Greenwood Press, 1985.
———, *1960–1984.* Westport, Conn., Greenwood Press, 1986.
Annotated entries in single alphabetical order of authors, titles, characters, settings. In emphasizing "books of recognized merit,"

some titles popular with children in different periods were omitted.

Emily Post's Etiquette, 14th ed. By Elizabeth L. Post. N.Y., Harper & Row, 1984.

Extraordinary Origins of Everyday Things. By Charles Panati. N.Y., Perennial Library/Harper & Row, 1987.
The beginnings of over five hundred diverse things. Indexed.

Festivals Sourcebook, 2d ed. Paul Wasserman, Managing Editor; Edmond L. Applebaum, Associate Editor. Detroit, Gale Research, 1984.
Chronological listing of festivals in the United States and Canada; event name, geographic, and subject indexes.

A Guide to Folktales in the English Language: Based on the Aarne-Thompson Classification System. By D. L. Ashliman. Westport, Conn., Greenwood Press, 1987.
Entries under classification numbers; includes thematic index with title/keyword structure, plot summaries, cross-references, and bibliography.

Intellectual Freedom Manual: ALA Office for Intellectual Freedom and Intellectual Freedom Committee. Chicago, American Library Association, 1989.

Manual for Writers of Term Papers, Theses, and Dissertations, 5th ed. By Kate L. Turabian. Revised and expanded by Bonnie Birtwistle Honigsblum. Chicago, University of Chicago Press, 1987.

Nonbook Media: Collection Management and User Services. Edited by John W. Ellison and Patricia Ann Coty. Chicago, American Library Association, 1987.
Chapters on "about twenty-two separate nonbook formats . . . to provide a source for the quick location of facts regarding these formats . . . contributed by practitioners who have had extensive experience with their respective formats" (Preface).

Oxford Dictionary of Quotations, 3d ed. N.Y., Oxford University Press, 1979.

Respectfully Quoted: A Dictionary of Quotations Requested from the Congressional Research Service. Edited by Suzy Platt. Washington, D.C., Library of Congress, 1989.

Robert's Rules of Order. By Henry M. Robert. New and enlarged edition by Sarah Corbin Robert. Glenview, Ill., Scott, Foresman, 1981.

Telling Stories to Children. By Sylvia Ziskind. N.Y., H. W. Wilson, 1976.

Webster's Standard American Style Manual. Springfield, Mass., Merriam-Webster, 1985.

5.
INDEXES, SERIALS, AND DIRECTORIES

Indexes, serials, and directories are among the most important sources of the library's reference collection. They are the keys to a vast assortment of information.

Indexes are as varied in format as are the kinds of information they disclose. The catalog of a library is an index to that library's holdings, just as the index in the back of a book may be the only key to information available in the library on a subject of interest. There are indexes to books, periodicals, newspapers, pamphlets, and microforms that locate and cite sources for every phase of humankind's recorded knowledge and activity.

Directories, too, abound in kind, size, and purpose. There are business, social, and professional directories; educational and institutional directories; and local, state, national, and international directories. Primarily, these are lists of people, organizations, and places. A directory may be a separate publication or a section of a work.

Serials are more difficult to describe. The introduction to *New Serial Titles* (q.v.) provides, from the *Anglo-American Cataloging Rules*, 2d ed. (Chicago, American Library Association, 1978), a definition of a serial as "A publication in any medium issued in successive parts bearing numerical or chronological designations and intended to be continued indefinitely. Serials include periodicals, newspapers, annuals (reports, yearbooks, etc.); the journals, memoirs, proceedings, transactions, etc., of societies; and numbered monographic series."

It must be remembered that, though this book chiefly presents printed sources as a foundation for understanding general reference sources, as stated in the introduction, most of the widely used and specialized indexes are now on microform, CD-ROM, and/or online.

Nomenclature is sometimes a cause of uncertainty and frustration. It is hoped that the reader will not worry needlessly about such "terminological inexactitude,"[1] but will concentrate on the content and

1. A phrase coined by Winston Churchill in a speech to the House of Commons, Feb. 22, 1906.

use of the sources. This chapter contains a small sampling. Every discipline has its own specialized indexes, serials, and directories. It is not the purpose here to delve into the reference sources of particular disciplines, but to examine some of the works that form the basic nucleus of a general reference collection.

Z
731
A53

AMERICAN LIBRARY DIRECTORY

N.Y., R. R. Bowker, 1923– . Annual.

The *Directory* was published biennially from 1908 until 1978, and has since then been issued annually. "The major section of the directory is a listing of public, academic, government and special libraries in the United States, and regions administered by it, and in Canada. Arranged geographically, the entries are alphabetized by state, region, or province; then by city; and finally by the institution or library name" (Preface, 41st ed., p. vii).

It is important to look carefully at the table of contents, because there are information sections in addition to the main directory. Read the preface, which provides an outline of the data included and the codes used to designate the types of libraries listed. This is followed by a sample entry, a library count (totals for major types of libraries in the United States, its territories, and Canada); and a key to symbols and abbreviations.

1. In the 1988–89 edition, turn to the entries (a) *Massachusetts: Cambridge: Harvard University*; note the detailed listings of special collections, major research units, library holdings, special interests, and automation info; and (b) *District of Columbia: Library of Congress*; see the many itemized holdings, such as the library's impressive music collection.

2. Where are the special libraries in your state that serve the blind and physically handicapped? Who provides the free recordings and Braille materials for these libraries?

3. What is the address of the National Library of Medicine? What are its publications?

4. Look through the section "Library Information" at the end of volume 2. It includes automation networks, library schools, national

interlibrary loan codes, libraries for the handicapped, and other library systems.

There is an index at the back of volume 2, preceded by an explanation of the order of listings.

Z
1219
B66

BOOK REVIEW DIGEST, 1905–
N.Y., H. W. Wilson, 1905– .

"The *Book Review Digest* (*BRD*) provides excerpts of and citations to reviews of current fiction and non-fiction in the English language" (Prefatory Note). It is published monthly, except February and July, with a bound annual cumulation. To be included in this publication, a book must be published or distributed in the United States or Canada and must receive a specific number of reviews in journals on the BRD list (nonfiction, 2 or more; fiction, 4 or more; juvenile fiction, 3 or more).

1. In one of the recent issues read the prefatory note, which is followed by a key to abbreviations and a list of periodicals indexed.

2. The complete bibliographical data and the reviews are found under the author's name in the main body of the index. Notice that nonfiction books list suggested Dewey classification numbers and subject headings, in addition to the price, ISBN, and Library of Congress catalog card number.

3. If a reader requests reviews of a biography of President Dwight D. Eisenhower written by David Eisenhower, you will find in the 1987 volume a *New York Times Book Review* summary, many citations of reviews, and four excerpts of reviews.

   In assisting a reader who has heard of a recent notable multi-volume biography of Field Marshall Bernard Montgomery and, though unsure of the title, thinks that it might be his nickname, *Monty*, if you start your search with the 1987 volume of the *BRD*, you will locate the work in the subject and title index under the biographee's full name and the title. The complete entry for the biography is under the author's name: Hamilton, Nigel. *Monty.* N.Y., McGraw-Hill, 1981–86. 3v.

4. A directory of publishers and distributors is at the end of each volume.

Additionally, there is:

Book Review Digest Author/Title Index, 1905–1974. N.Y., H. W. Wilson, 1976. 4v.

——, *1975–1984.* N.Y., H. W. Wilson, 1986.

JK
1011
U5

CONGRESSIONAL DIRECTORY, 1809–
Washington, D.C., U.S. Government
Printing Office, 1809– .

This is a most useful and important reference work. The *Directory* provides information on people and agencies in all branches of the federal government, and on people in related agencies. Notice on the title page that, in addition to the year of publication, the *Directory* is identified by the session of Congress (e.g., 1987–88:100th Congress) and the date it convened. There are notes at the beginning of the volume designating the changes occurring after the most recent election.

There is a detailed table of contents; scan it for a better understanding of what is included. See also the subject and name indexes in the back of the book.

1. The first section is biographical. "Biographies are based on information furnished or authorized by the respective senators and representatives" (p. 3). The first sketch is of the vice-president, followed by the senators and representatives by state and delegates from the territories. The representatives are presented in numerical order by districts represented. In the heading for each district, the counties included in that district are given with their total population. The biographical sketch for each congressperson includes party affiliation, city of residence, birth place and date, education, military service, career and family information, and political offices held.

2. The second section lists state delegations. Under the states, which are listed in alphabetical order, the names of senators and representatives are given with, for the representatives, the number of the district represented. Note that the Democrats are identified in roman type, Republicans in italic.

3. The third section is an alphabetical list of members of the Senate and House of Representatives, with name, district, address, office room, telephone number, and staff members, provided.

4. Continue looking through this comprehensive compilation. The coverage of the legislative branch includes the officers, terms of service, and committee assignments of its members. After this you will find sections entitled "Statistical Information," "The Capitol," "The Executive Branch," "Independent Agencies," "The Judiciary," "The District of Columbia," "International Organizations," "Foreign Diplomatic Representatives and Foreign Consular Offices in the United States, "The United States Diplomatic and Consular Offices," and "Press, Radio, and Television Galleries." Maps of congressional districts are also included. (Did you notice the section "Capital Floor Plans"?)

5. To gain experience in the use of the *Directory*, look through the information given for:
   a. One of the departments of the executive branch, such as the Department of State or Department of Justice;
   b. An independent agency, such as the National Aeronautics and Space Administration or the National Commission on Libraries and Information Science;
   c. The diplomatic service. What are the addresses in Washington, D.C. of the embassies of Canada and Denmark? Does the United States have an embassy or consular office in Switzerland?
   d. The history of the legislative branch. Who was the first Speaker of the House of Representatives? What was the opening date of the first session?

HS	**ENCYCLOPEDIA OF ASSOCIATIONS**
17	Detroit, Gale Research, 1956– . Annual.
G334	

"The *Encyclopedia of Associations*, Volume 1, first published in 1956, is the only comprehensive source of detailed information concerning nonprofit American membership organizations of national scope. In it can be found details on the location, size, objectives, and many other essential aspects of . . . trade and professional associations, social welfare and public affairs organizations, labor unions, fraternal and patriotic organizations, and other types of groups consisting of voluntary members" (Introduction).

The *Encyclopedia* consists of volume 1, *National Organizations of the United States*; volume 2, *Geographic and Executive Indexes* (covering material in volume 1); volume 3, *New Associations and Projects*; and volume 4, *International Organizations*.

"Volume 1 of the *Encyclopedia of Associations* is published in three separately bound parts. Parts 1 and 2 contain descriptive entries arranged in 18 subject sections, as outlined on the 'Contents' pages. Within each subject section, entries are arranged alphabetically by the principal subject keyword appearing in boldface in, or following, the organization's name. Part 3 of the *Encyclopedia* comprises an alphabetical Name and Keyword Index providing access to all organizations listed in Parts 1 and 2 as well as to additional information" (Introduction).

1. In the section "How to Use This Book," there is a large sample entry with an explanation of each item that appears in an entry. An important part of each entry is the keyword, which refers to the organization's field of activity. In the comprehensive, alphabetical index, you can look up organizations under either the keyword or the name.

2. In volume 1, part 1, look through the table of contents. Would you expect to find *librarians* and *libraries* under *cultural organizations*?

3. What is the Wolf Trap Foundation? Where is it located?
   How many members does the American Library Association have? What is its budget? Are the dates and places of its Annual conferences given?

4. In volume 1, part 3, in "How to Use This Book," refer to the instructions on the name and keyword index. The use of this index is essential to the efficient location of an entry. To confirm this, look up *librarians*. Note that some of the organizations are listed as defunct. What does an asterisk before the entry number indicate? At the bottom of alternate, odd-numbered pages, there is a key to abbreviations used to identify other sources of information about the organizations cited. See the entries for the Association of International Libraries and the multiple listings for the National Commission on Libraries and Information Science.

A1	**ESSAY AND GENERAL LITERATURE**
3	**INDEX, 1900–**
E75	N.Y., H. W. Wilson, 1934– .

Librarians, often presented with a mind-swamping range of questions at a busy reference desk, have traditionally turned for help to a source called "analytics," or information card files prepared by the staff. The *Essay and General Literature Index* reduces the need for these, helps in many otherwise frustrating searches, and encourages maximum use of the library's collection. It is principally an author and subject index to collections of essays, with emphasis on the humanities and social sciences, but includes a wide range of fields.

The *Index* is published semiannually with a paper issue in June, an annual cumulation, and a five-year cumulation.

1. The directions for use, found in the front of each volume, are simple and easy to follow. The "List of Books Indexed" at the back of each volume must be consulted for complete bibliographic information on the collections. Following the list there is a "Directory of Publishers and Distributors."

2. As examples of the listings for major authors, look up Eugene O'Neill and Sophocles in the 1980–84 edition. There are entries for works about the authors, individual works, stage history, influence, etc. One of the essays on Sophocles is:
   Easterling, P. E. Character in Sophocles.
      In Greek tragedy, ed. by E. Segal p138–45.
   Because the essay by Easterling was published in the book by Segal, you would check in your library's catalog under Segal or the title of his book. You will find complete bibliographic information for the book in the "List of Books Indexed."

3. "Essay" is a rather limiting term for this index, as the works cited include what researchers consider articles, chapters in books, reviews, etc. Additionally, it includes many subjects that would not be classed as "general literature," such as civil rights, nuclear facilities, analyses of Supreme Court cases, etc. Look through the latest cumulation of this index to learn the variety of subjects listed. There is a generous provision of *see* and *see also* references.

Z
6951
A97

GALE DIRECTORY OF PUBLICATIONS:
An Annual Guide to Newspapers, Magazines,
Journals, and Related Publications
Detroit, Gale Research, 1987–   . 2v. Annual.

This directory has had several titles (principally and popularly known earlier as *Ayer's*) and publisher changes in its long and respected history, but remains a standard, indispensable source. It provides "ready access in a geographic arrangement to basic information about newspapers, magazines, journals, and similar publications issued in the United States and Canada. . . . State and province sections begin with a page or two of descriptive information including a general description of the state/province and various types of statistical information. Brief facts are also given for cities" (Introduction).

Certain types of publications are omitted, such as those issued by elementary and high schools, houses of worship, and most internal publications ("house organs").

Each entry for the publications includes the frequency of issue, date established, subscription price, size of column and page, advertising rates, circulation, and the names and addresses of editors and publishers.

1. It is essential to study the sample entry and the indexing sample given in the introductory pages. The table of contents offers an outline of the arrangement.

2. As an example of the data provided for states see the entry for Indiana, which gives the name of the capital, location, physical description, climate, population, economy, counties, universities, and statistics on newspapers and periodicals. See also the listings for the District of Columbia; Lexington, Kentucky; and Toronto, Ontario, Canada.

3. When was the *Washington Post* established? What is its circulation? How does the cost of a subscription compare to that of the *New York Times*?

   Is the address for the publisher of *Gourmet: The Magazine of Good Living* different from that listed for subscription inquiries?

   Where is the periodical *Maclean's* published? How often is it issued?

4. Read the table of contents of volume 2. See the collection of maps of the states and provinces, with insets of major cities and the roster of newspaper feature editors. The cross-reference indexes are a helpful feature. The multiple categories of publications are listed by subject or type, as foreign language, newsletters, college, trade, technical and professional, daily, weekly, etc.

   At the end of the volume, the alphabetical title and keyword index lists all publications cited in the *Directory.*

PN
1021
G7

GRANGER'S INDEX TO POETRY:
Indexing Anthologies Published through
June 30, 1985, 8th ed.
Edited by William F. Barnhardt
Completely revised and enlarged
N.Y., Columbia University Press, 1986. xxxiii, 2,014p.

Granger's Index to Poetry was first published in 1904 and is recognized as a standard and indispensable reference work. Its chief use is to identify and locate poems published in anthologies. *Granger's* is divided into three indexes: title and first line, author, and subject.

1. Read the explanatory notes. These are followed by a list of abbreviations used and the key to symbols, which identify the anthologies indexed. Each entry in the title and first line index is followed by alphabetical symbols for the anthologies in which the work appears. The title and first line index is the principal index and must be used in connection with both the author and the subject index. The symbols for the anthologies are not cited in the author and subject indexes.

2. If a reader tells you that he or she wishes to find a poem, but does not remember the poet, the title, or lines, only that it is about St. Francis of Assisi appearing before several young mental patients in a garden, you begin a search in the subject index. As in the use of most indexes, you should try to think of as many related subjects as possible. A search under *St. Francis of Assisi, gardens, hospitals,* and *patients* does not produce the described poem, but in reading the entries under *mental illness* you find it—"The Mental Hospital Garden," by William Carlos Williams—with the symbol for one anthology. The symbol must be matched with the title of the collection entered in the front of the volume. You complete the process by looking up the collection in the library catalog.

   It does require patience. The librarian should assure the patron that although the method seems complex or time consuming, it is really the shortest and most effective route to finding a poem in an anthology.

3. You have to look through the subject index to appreciate the number and variety of categories. There are poems about immigrants, flowers, San Francisco, California, and Abraham Lincoln, and there are lists of anthologies containing love poems, story poems, etc.

4. Recommendations of anthologies are made for primary, or priority, acquisition and for additional acquisitions. These are indicated by the use of asterisks—two for primary and one for additional acquisitions.

Z
666
L69

LIBRARY LITERATURE:
An Index to Library and Information
Science, 1921–32–
N.Y., H. W. Wilson, 1934– .

Library Literature is an alphabetical author and subject index to books, periodicals, pamphlets, films, filmstrips, and microforms. It is published bimonthly, with annual and two-year cumulations. Any subject concerned with libraries and librarianship is considered appropriate for inclusion.

Read the explanatory notes, which are followed by sample entries, abbreviations of periodicals indexed, periodicals indexed, and abbreviations.

1. Turn to a subject of continuing, crucial interest to librarians— *Censorship.* Under the heading there is a listing of *see also* references and subheadings by state. Note that several of the entries were published in the *Newsletter on Intellectual Freedom,* a bimonthly publication of the American Library Association.

2. Select a topic of interest to see what is currently being published, as *CD-ROM, Medical Libraries,* and *Children's Literature.* Keep up with the progress of the profession by referring to articles cited under such headings as *Personnel, Salaries; Librarianship—Philosophical Aspects;* and *Books and Reading.*

3. Book reviews are listed in a separate section at the end of the volumes.

PN
161
L52

LITERARY MARKET PLACE.
LMP: The Directory of American Book
Publishing, with Names & Numbers
N.Y., R. R. Bowker, 1940– . Annual.

The comprehensiveness of this annual directory of American book publishing and allied fields can be appreciated by reading the table of contents. "Information in *LMP* is grouped into fifteen general categories as indicated in the table of contents. Each sub-category is assigned a section number. Most of the sections contain a brief annotation describing in detail that section's content, entry criteria and particular arrangements" (Preface, p. vii).

1. The opening section is a listing of book publishers, first given in alphabetical order. The entries include the parent company (when applicable), address, telephone number, management and editorial personnel, ISBN and SAN, types of publications, number published in the preceding year, date founded, and imprints. The publishers are relisted in sections classified by geographical location, fields of activity, and subject matter. The lists by activity and subject matter are very helpful for answering questions, for example, about which houses publish mysteries, poetry, or books in industrial technology, science, or the humanities.

   Can you find a list of firms that publish children's books? We are accustomed to having cross-references provided. Here you will have to search under associated subjects.

2. Scan other sections of interest, such as literary or illustration agents, writers' conferences and workshops, and literary awards, contests, and grants. Note that editorial services are classified by fields of activity.

   There is a listing of wholesalers to schools and libraries. Every aspect of book manufacture, such as paper, type, and binding, is represented.

   Another section of professional interest lists the recent multiple book-trade acquisitions and mergers.

3. In the 1988 edition, "the Indexes to Sections and Advertisers have been moved to the back of the directory. A toll-free phone number index for publishers has been added and follows immediately after Names and Numbers. These four sections comprise the yellow page section of the book. A new section (73) has been added to list those periodicals which, in addition to carrying book reviews, are known to excerpt and serialize books or are vehicles for book trade advertising" (p. vii).

A1
21
N45

NEW YORK TIMES INDEX: A Book of Record
v. 1– , 1913–
N.Y. Times, 1913– .

The current series of the *Index* has been published continuously since January, 1913. All volumes of the previous series (September 1851–

1912) are available. It is published semimonthly with quarterly cumulations and an annual cumulated volume. The title page carries the statement "The Master-Key to the News since 1851." The *Index* "contains abstracts of the significant news, editorial matter and special features published in the newspaper, daily and Sunday. . . . Headings and their subdivisions, if any, are arranged alphabetically; the entries under them are arranged chronologically. Each entry is followed by a precise reference—date, page and column—to the item which it summarizes" (p. ii). For example, if the citation for an entry reads My 6, IV, 3:4, the item was published on May 6, section 4, page 3, column 4. The section is always expressed as a Roman numeral, even when the newspaper uses a letter designation in the Monday–Friday issues, as A = I, B = II.

Read the explanations on the use of the *Index* and see the key to abbreviations in the front of a bound volume. Note that the single capital letters in the entries are indicators of the length of news stories: (L) means a long story over three columns; (M) means a medium-sized story of one to three columns; and (S) means a short story less than one column.

Remember that the date represents the date on which a news item appeared in the *New York Times,* not the date on which the event occurred.

1. In the 1988 annual volume, look at the listings under *children and youth* and *medicine.* You will find multiple cross-references. A revealing long list is under *banks and banking.* Entries of unusual interest are set in boldface type.

2. Citations of book reviews extend over several pages. Select one of the titles to learn whether you could find a reference to the book review in the *Index* under the author or title.

3. There are also special subject indexes to the *New York Times,* as the *Personal Name Index* and the *Cumulative Subject and Personal Name Index: Women.*

Z
5781
P53

PLAY INDEX, 1983–1987
Edited by Juliette Yaakov and John Greenfieldt
N.Y., H. W. Wilson, 1988. 522p.

This seventh edition of the *Play Index* series, which was first published in 1953, lists about four thousand plays representing various forms of theatrical works published in the five-year period.

The contents are clearly described in the directions for use. The *Index* is divided into four parts. Part 1 is the author, title, and subject index in a single alphabetical listing. The author entry includes the name of the author, title of the work, a brief descriptive note, the number of acts and scenes, the size of the cast, the number of sets required, and the publisher. If you look up a play by title or subject, you must refer to the author entry for full information. The symbols in the left margin indicate performance/audience level: *c* for children through grade 6 and *y* for young people in grades 7–10, approximately. See the sample entry.

As explained in the introduction to part 2, Cast Analysis, the section is designed to locate plays by number of players or readers. It is divided into six listings: all male, all female, and mixed cast, puppet plays, unidentified, and variable cast. "Unidentified cast is used for non-human characters, and variable cast is used when roles can be acted by either male or female characters, or when an actor can take several parts, so that the exact number of the cast is not clearly ascertainable." Under each type of cast, the arrangement is from the small to the large cast of over thirty-five characters.

Part 3 is an author-title list of collections indexed. Remember that publishers of single plays are listed in part 1 in the author entries.

Part 4 is a directory of publishers and distributors.

1. Look up the entry for Neil Simon's *Chapter Two*. Read the descriptive note, which is followed by the number of acts and scenes, the size of cast, and the number of sets. Under the entry for Simon's *Biloxi Blues*, there are three single publications of the play cited, and one listing in a collection. Note that the collection is the annual series, *Best Plays*, and that the plays in that series are condensations.

2. Look through the *Index* to learn the range of the multiple subjects: comedies, mysteries, the West (U.S.), Spanish drama, monologues, etc.

Z
7163
P9

**PUBLIC AFFAIRS INFORMATION
SERVICE BULLETIN**
N.Y., PAIS, 1915– .

The *Public Affairs Information Service Bulletin*, usually referred to as *PAIS*, is issued monthly, with three quarterly cumulations and an annual bound volume with an author index. "The *PAIS* indexes list publications on all subjects that bear on contemporary public issues and the making and evaluation of public policy, irrespective of source or traditional disciplinary boundaries. ... The listings encompass printed materials in all formats: periodical articles, books, government documents, and the reports of public and private organizations" (*PAIS* Selection Policy). It is an alphabetically arranged subject index. For author entries, you must refer to the annual bound volume.

1. Be certain to read the user's guide at the front of an issue; it gives examples of the various entries. This is followed by a key to bibliographical symbols and abbreviations, a key to periodical references, and a directory of publishers and organizations.

2. As examples of the wide diversity of topics, look up in the latest annual volume the entries competition; child welfare; insurance, health; space, outer; and immigration and emigration. Each bibliographic entry appears under from one to four subject headings, with generous cross-references. In an annual volume, under *libraries*, note that the sources include books, journals, and government publications, with many subdivisions and *see also* references.

The Foreign Language Index (N.Y., PAIS, 1972–), a companion to the *PAIS Bulletin*, indexes materials on economics and public affairs published in languages other than English. The *PAIS International Database* is the online version of *PAIS Bulletin* and *PAIS Foreign Language Index*.

A1
3
R48

READERS' GUIDE TO PERIODICAL LITERATURE, 1900–
N.Y., H. W. Wilson, 1905– .

Of all the indexes found in libraries, the *Readers' Guide* is probably the best known and most frequently consulted. It is published in paperbound issues twice a month in March, April, September, October, and December, and once a month in January, February, May through August, and November. The February, May through August, and November issues are quarterly cumulations. There is an annual clothbound cumulation. The *Readers' Guide* is an index to periodicals of general, popular interest.

Articles are listed by author, subject, and title in a single alphabet.

1. If you are not already skilled in the use of the *Readers' Guide*, study the suggestions for use and the sample entries provided for clarification, the abbreviations of periodicals indexed, lists of periodicals indexed, and abbreviations.

2. Most requests from readers for assistance involve a subject. Although there are ample cross-references, the librarian frequently needs to be resourceful in associating and checking appropriate subject headings. When first introduced to the *Readers' Guide*, readers may become confused or discouraged in attempting to find a subject listed as a subdivision or subheading. As an example, for information on incidents involving U.S. Navy ships ordered to the Persian Gulf in 1987–88, the researcher must find within the many pages of headings, beginning with *United States*, the entry: *United States. Navy*. Under that entry there are *see also* references, followed by citations of articles on the general subject, then by subheadings in alphabetical order, as *appropriations and expenditures, civilian employees*, to *forces in the Persian Gulf region*. The 1987 volume includes the article:
   Swept up in the tides of the Gulf. H. Anderson.
   il *Newsweek* 110:40–2 Ag 10 '87
   The article is entered by title, is written by H. Anderson, is illustrated, and appears in the periodical *Newsweek*, volume 110, on pages 40–42 of the August 10, 1987, issue.

3. If you wish to locate a review of a movie, you must look under the subject heading *motion picture reviews—single works* for the complete citation. The list of movies is in alphabetical order. For a review of a stage play, look under the playwright's name, or, if this is not known, under the title, which will refer you to the playwright. Titles of plays are found under the subject heading *theater reviews—single works*, but again you must refer to the entry for the author to obtain complete information. There is a separate section for book reviews, in alphabetical order by author, at the end of each issue.

4. An additional publication, the *Abridged Readers' Guide*, which is exactly what the name implies, is designed for school and very small libraries. The *Readers' Guide*, as is true for many of the H. W.

Wilson indexes, is sold to libraries on a subscription basis using a system that equalizes the cost of the service to libraries of varying sizes and budgets. A full description of this system can be found in the latest catalog of the company's publications.

Readers' Guide Abstracts. N.Y., H. W. Wilson, 1984–   .
Summaries of selected articles indexed in *Readers' Guide to Periodical Literature.*

Z
5917
S5

SHORT STORY INDEX: An Index to Stories in Collections and Periodicals
N.Y., H. W. Wilson, 1953–   .

The *Short Story Index* is published annually, with five-year cumulations. The series indexes stories in collections and periodicals in a single alphabet arrangement by author, title, and subject. The author entry is the complete entry. The sections of each volume include the main index, a list of collections indexed, a directory of publishers and distributors, and a directory of periodicals.

1. Study the directions for use, which immediately precede the index.

2. As an example for the possible use of this index, a patron might tell you that she has seen a movie that very much impressed her. It was based on a short story, but she didn't recognize or remember the author's name. The story is about the final adjustment, the late appreciation of the relationship of an elderly man and his very ill wife. The only other clue she has is that the title has the word "riddle" in it.
   If the librarian doesn't recognize the work from the description given, this type of question usually requires a patient search with no guaranteed result. But, for this example, refer to the cumulated volume for 1974–78. There is no entry for the subject *riddles*. If you think of subjects related to the theme, you might look under *marriage* and its subdivisions. There is no title that includes "riddle." If you look under *wives*, you will find a *see* reference to *husband and wife*, but not a possible title. You might then consider a parallel theme and search under *old age*. The list of stories includes: Olsen, Tillie. "Tell me a riddle." Two anthologies are cited by editors and titles. The complete bibliographic data is given in the list of collections indexed at the back of the book.

3. The number and variety of subjects indexed are fascinating, and even include librarians! For science fiction buffs, note the pages of entries under *space*, with its multiple subdivisions.

Z
6941
U5

ULRICH'S INTERNATIONAL PERIODICALS DIRECTORY, 1988–89, Now Including Irregular Serials and Annuals, 27th ed.
The Bowker International Serials Database.
N.Y., R. R. Bowker, 1989. 3v.

Since the first edition of this directory in 1932, there have been many changes in format, arrangement, and coverage. *Ulrich's* is published annually in three volumes and lists over 70,000 international periodicals. It now includes the directory *Irregular Serials and Annuals*, which had been separately published since 1967.

Preceding the main text there are directions for use and several other features of interest to librarians. Some of these include tables showing money symbols; a list of subject headings in English, French, German, and Spanish; abstracting and indexing services; country publication codes; and a cross-index to subjects.

1. Study the user's guide and the sample entry shown at the beginning of volume 1. One of the items in the entry is the ISSN, the International Standard Serial Number, which is explained on pages xxxvii–xxxviii.

2. There is a title index in volume 3. If you were asked about a periodical entitled *Hospital Week*, by referring to the title index you would find that the entry is in the section for cessations in volume 3.

3. *Ulrich's* includes U.S. government periodicals. If a subject heading for these eludes you, try *public administration*.

4. What is the subscription rate for *Architectural Digest*? Can you find it under the subject, *Architecture*?

5. This is an excellent source for learning what journals are available in specific fields. As examples, look up nutrition and dietetics, library and information sciences, medical sciences (with the multiple subdivisions and specialties), and industrial relations.

6. Volume 3 contains serials available online with a vendor listing; cessations; an index to publications of international organizations; and an ISSN and title index.

Z
6945
U45

UNION LIST OF SERIALS IN LIBRARIES OF THE UNITED STATES AND CANADA, 3d ed.
Edited by Edna Brown Titus
N.Y., H. W. Wilson, 1965. 5v.

A union list of periodicals is a catalog that includes the names of libraries (local, regional, national, or international) in which complete or partial sets of the periodicals can be located.

This third edition is a cumulated list of the previous editions, and includes thousands of additional titles. It is important to remember that although the third edition was published in 1965, the serials included began publication before 1950. For later serials and the names of the libraries that own them, refer to *New Serial Titles* (q.v.).

1. Examine the first few pages of one of the five volumes to understand the purpose of the list, its arrangement, and how it is to be used. Note the list of the cooperating libraries and the identifying code letters for each. The code letters for the Los Angeles Public Library are CL; CPT represents "Cal Tech," the California Institute of Technology in Pasadena. What do the letters in parentheses represent? CL has (L*) after its name, and "Cal Tech" has (L*, P.M.).

2. The preface reviews the history of the *Union List of Serials* and its predecessors. The financial support of the Council on Library Resources was an important factor in the success of this enormous undertaking. The introduction provides additional information regarding the procedures and policies followed in the development of the project. Note the list of types of serials that are generally excluded, such as law reports and digests and United Nations publications. Be sure to study the explanation of the sample entries before you attempt to use the *List*.

3. If you wished to see copies of the *American Mercury* and didn't know if it had ceased publication, you would find in the first volume the entry:
    AMERICAN Mercury. NY. 1, Ja 1924, +D 1951 as New American Mercury. Absorbed Common Sense F1946
    From this entry you learn that the *American Mercury*, started in 1924, was still being published at the time of the *Union List* publication. From December 1950 until March 1951 it was called the *New American Mercury*. In February 1946, it absorbed the magazine called *Common Sense*. There is a long list of libraries having

files of varying completeness. Those that have "1 +" in the entry have the complete run from volume 1 to date.

The *Union List of Serials* ceased publication with the third edition of 1965. However, the Library of Congress continued the publication with *New Serial Titles* (q.v.) for periodicals begun after 1950.

Z
6945
N44

NEW SERIAL TITLES: A Union List of Serials Held by Libraries in the United States and Canada
Prepared under the Sponsorship of the Joint Committee on the Union List of Serials
Washington, D.C., Library of Congress, 1953–   .

The list of *New Serial Titles* is a continuation of the *Union List of Serials* (q.v.). *New Serial Titles* began in January 1953, appearing in eight monthly and three quarterly issues and annual cumulations. It includes serials first published after December 31, 1949, that were received by the Library of Congress and cooperating libraries. In 1973, a four-volume cumulative edition for 1950–70, with thousands of revisions and additional locations, was published with the complete listing converted to a computer database.

The entries in *NST* cite title and title changes; first and, if applicable, last dates of publication; what constitutes a complete set; holdings of cooperating libraries; symbols for libraries holding the serials; and ISSN.

1. Read the preface of a current issue for a brief background and an explanation of the part the CONSER Project played in the publication. Review the arrangement of the work and the explanation of the symbols and abbreviations.

2. What information can you obtain about the *School Library Journal*? When did it begin publication? Who is the publisher? What other title did it once have?

   In what libraries could you locate issues of the *Medieval Monograph* series published by York [England] University?

CONCORDANCES

A concordance is defined as "an alphabetical list of the important words used in a book or by a particular writer with references to the passages in which they occur" (*Webster's New World Dictionary,* q.v.). It is an index that may be overlooked in general reference searches because it has been identified as a specialized or scholarly source. However, concordances to the Bible and to works of Shakespeare are in many small- and medium-sized libraries where they are useful in identifying quotations not found in general or limited quotation books. Large research libraries would have, additionally, concordances to the works of many major authors.

1. If a reader wanted references to the use of a handkerchief by the evil Iago in Shakespeare's *Othello,* by looking up the key word, handkerchief, in a concordance to Shakespeare's works, you would find several listings, one of which is: Act III, scene 3, line 306 (citations may vary in the use of Roman and Arabic numerals). This same precise form of listing would be found for a quotation from the Bible, citing book, chapter, and verse.
   Examples of concordances:
   Complete Concordance to the Bible (Douay version). By Newton Wayland Thompson and Raymond Stock. St. Louis, Herder, 1945.
   Exhaustive Concordance of the Bible. By James Strong. London, Hodder, 1894; N.Y., Abingdon, 1980.
   Nelson's Complete Concordance of the New American Bible. Stephen J. Hartdegen, General Editor. Nashville, Nelson, 1977.
   Nelson's Complete Concordance of the Revised Standard Version Bible. Compiled under the Supervision of John W. Ellison. N.Y., Nelson, 1957.
   Harvard Concordance to Shakespeare. By Marvin Spevack. Cambridge, Mass. Belknap Press of Harvard University, 1973.
   New and Complete Concordance or Verbal Index to Words . . . in the Dramatic Works of Shakespeare. By John Bartlett. London, Macmillan, 1894; Reprint: N.Y., St. Martin's Press, 1953.

Look carefully through a concordance to learn the detailed information and possible uses provided.

INDEXES, SERIALS, AND DIRECTORIES

Additional Titles

American Universities and Colleges. N.Y., W. de Gruyter, 1928– .
Quadrennial. Sponsored by the American Council on Education.
Publisher varies.

Audio Video Market Place: A Multimedia Guide. N.Y., R. R. Bowker,
1969– . Annual.

Barron's Profiles of American Colleges, 16th ed. Compiled and edited
by the College Division of Barron's Educational Series. Woodbury,
N.Y., Barron's Educational Series, 1988.

Book Review Index, 1965– . Detroit, Gale Research, 1965– . Bimonthly; annual cumulations.

————: *A Master Cumulation, 1965–1984.* Edited by Gary C. Tarbert
and Barbara Beach. Detroit, Gale Research, 1985. 10v.

————: *Reference Books, 1965–1984.* Edited by Barbara Beach. Detroit, Gale Research, 1986.
"More than 87,000 citations to reviews of about 40,000 reference
books."

*Children's Literature Awards and Winners: A Directory of Prizes,
Authors, and Illustrators,* 2d ed. Compiled and edited by Dolores
Blythe Jones. Detroit, Gale Research, 1988. A Neal-Schuman pub-
lication.

College Handbook. N.Y., College Entrance Examination Board,
1941– . Biennial.

Contemporary Literary Criticism. Detroit, Gale Research, 1973– .
Series. Citations with "excerpts from criticism of the works of
today's novelists, poets, playwrights and other creative writers."

Facts on File: A Weekly World News Digest. N.Y., Facts on File,
1940– .

Index to Children's Plays in Collections, 3d ed. Edited by Beverly R.
Trefny. Metuchen, N.J., Scarecrow Press, 1986.

*Index to Fairy Tales, 1973–1977; Including Folklore, Legends and
Myths in Collections.* Compiled by Norma Olin Ireland. 4th sup-
plement to Mary Huse Eastman's *Index.* Westwood, Mass., F. W.
Faxon, 1979.

*Index to Illustrations of Living Things outside North America: Where
to Find Pictures of Flora and Fauna.* Compiled and edited by Lucille
Thompson Munz and Nedra G. Slauson. Hamden Conn., Shoe
String Press, 1981.

Index to Illustrations of the Natural World: Where to Find Pictures of the Living Things of North America. Compiled by John W. Thompson and edited by Nedra G. Slauson. Hamden, Conn., Shoe String Press, 1983.

Index to Poetry for Children and Young People: 1982–1987. Compiled by G. Meredith Blackburn III and Lorraine A. Blackburn. N.Y., H. W. Wilson, 1989.

Series began in 1942, compiled by John E. and Sara W. Brewton, with two supplements; subsequent editions in five-year cumulations. Indexed by title, subject, author, and first line entries, with analyses of books indexed.

Magazine Index Plus on InfoTrac. San Mateo, Calif., Information Access, 1980– . Monthly.

Mystery Index: Subjects, Settings, and Sleuths of 10,000 Titles. By Steven Olderr. Chicago, American Library Association, 1987.

Indexed by main entries, titles, subjects, type of detective, etc.

National Directory of Addresses and Telephone Numbers. Kirkland, Wash., General Information, 1981– .

Includes government, national and international corporations, banks, colleges, embassies, hospitals, etc.

Standard Periodical Directory, 12th ed. N.Y., Oxbridge Communications, 1989.

Data on "65,000 periodicals" published in the United States and Canada, including newspapers, by subject; title index.

The Storyteller's Sourcebook: A Subject, Title, and Motif Index to Folklore Collections for Children. Edited by Margaret Read MacDonald. A Neal-Schuman Book. Detroit, Gale Research, 1982.

Vertical File Index. N.Y., H. W. Wilson, 1935– . Monthly except August.

Indexes selected pamphlets and inexpensive paperbacks on topics of popular interest.

World of Winners. Detroit, Gale Research, 1988.

A directory of winners of "most significant" awards; honors and prizes in all fields.

Worldwide Chamber of Commerce Directory. Loveland, Colo., 1965– . Annual.

Addresses of chambers of commerce for each state in the United States and foreign countries, including foreign offices in the United States and U.S. Congress rosters by state.

6.
BIBLIOGRAPHIES

The term *bibliography* means different things to different people. A bibliography may be a simple list of books consulted by a high school student in writing a term paper or a universal catalog that lists books and nonbook materials in libraries or private collections all over the world. Despite these extremes, the lists have three things in common: purpose, form, and unity.

Language, our greatest invention, is simultaneously our stabilizer and an instrument for change. *Bibliography*, like other words in our active vocabulary, has become wider in scope and more flexible in meaning. The word comes from the Greek *bibliographia*, the writing of books. The change does not weaken the term; rather, it enriches it.

We need to be aware of a number of definitions of *bibliography*. *The Random House Dictionary of the English Language* (q.v.) offers the following definitions:

1. A complete or selective list of works compiled upon some common principle, as authorship, subject, place of publication, or printer;
2. A list of source materials that are used or consulted in the preparation of a work or that are referred to in the text;
3. A branch of library science dealing with the history, physical description, comparison, and classification of books and other works.

Through bibliographies the user may learn the kinds, amounts, and locations of materials available. A bibliography should include accurate information on the name of the author, editor, compiler, or other issuing body; the full title of the work; the name of the publisher; and the place and date of publication. It may include the collation (physical characteristics of the work), the price, an annotation, citations of reviews, the number of editions or reprints, and the names of libraries or other collections in which a particular item is located. Bibliographies may be organized by subject, locale, kind of material, chronology, author, title, series, or any way that serves the purpose of the bibliographer.

The form of the bibliography is important for accuracy and for convenience to the user. An informal or haphazard list of items that contains partial or varying citations is a travesty of a true bibliography. The form should follow a systematic pattern throughout.

For the bibliophile, researcher, bookseller, scholar, and librarian, a bibliography is the center around which related activities revolve and develop.

Z
1035.1
A55

**AMERICAN REFERENCE BOOKS
ANNUAL, 1970–**
Edited by Bohdan S. Wynar
Englewood, Colo., Libraries Unlimited, 1970–   .

The *ARBA* provides "reviews of the complete spectrum of English language reference books published in the United States and Canada during a single year" (Introduction). Some exceptions are annuals, such as yearbooks, almanacs, and annually updated encyclopedias, which are reviewed at intervals of three to five years. Reference books not reviewed include those of less than forty-eight pages, those produced by vanity presses or the author as publisher, and some materials produced by library staffs for their own use.

Reviews written by subject specialists from U.S. and Canadian libraries and universities are signed; those by members of the *ARBA* staff are not signed.

1. Read the introduction for an overview of the coverage. Some reviews cite additional reviews that appeared in library journals. The lists of journals and abbreviations used follow the table of contents.

2. Look over the table of contents to learn the arrangement of the subject classes. Turn to the sections on general reference works and library science and another subject of your choice. Read several of the reviews. Most are well-balanced, objective appraisals.

3. There is an author-title and a subject index. Note that the numbers after the entries refer to entry numbers rather than to page numbers.

    The *Index to American Reference Books Annual* (1970–74; 1975–79; 1980–84) provides a cumulative author, title, and subject index to the annual editions.

Z
1002
B595

**BIBLIOGRAPHIC INDEX: A Cumulative
Bibliography of Bibliographies, 1937–**
N.Y., H. W. Wilson, 1938– .

The *Bibliographic Index* is issued in April and August, with a bound cumulation in December. It "is a subject list of bibliographies published separately or appearing as parts of books, pamphlets, and periodicals. Selection is made from bibliographies which have fifty or more citations. The Index concentrates on titles in English, other Germanic languages, and the Romance languages" (Prefatory note).

1. Review the sample entries for books, pamphlets, and periodicals, with the explanation for each given at the front of each issue. These are followed by keys to general abbreviations and periodical abbreviations.

   For the full names and addresses of the publishers of cited works, you are referred to the directory in the *Cumulative Book Index* (q.v.).

2. There are numerous cross-references to guide the user to the subject headings used; if searching for a bibliography on desegregation in education, you are directed by a *see* reference to school integration. For some subjects, one is merely referred to *see issues* of a particular periodical, indicating that a bibliography is included in each issue. Look at *labor and laboring classes.* There is a cross-reference to *see issues* of the *International Labour Review* and the *Monthly Labor Review.* Under *children's literature* there are a number of periodicals cited, among them *School Library Journal* and *Booklist.*

   See references appear in every issue. *See also* references appear only in the annual volumes.

3. If a researcher asks for a bibliography on the liberal vs. conservative opinions of the U.S. Supreme Court, the 1987 edition of the *Index* lists a book by Lee Epstein titled *Conservatives in Court* (University of Tennessee Press, 1985, p. 176–91). The paging is for the bibliography.

Z
1215
B972

BOOKS IN PRINT, 1948–
N.Y., R. R. Bowker, 1948– . 7v. Annual.

Books in Print is produced from the database of the R. R. Bowker Company and gives librarians, booksellers, publishers, and other book users access to the latest bibliographic ordering information. *BIP* lists books published or exclusively distributed in the United States. The 1988–89 edition lists over 750,000 titles. Refer to the introductory pages to learn what type of books are excluded, such as Bibles, government publications, and audiovisual materials.

Books in Print, started in 1948, is an indispensable source for the librarian. In the seven-volume set, volumes 1 through 3 provide the author index, in alphabetical order by author, editor, or compiler; volumes 4 through 6 form the title index, in alphabetical arrangement. Volume 7 is the publishers index.

1. Read the section entitled "How to Use *Books in Print.*" A key to abbreviations immediately precedes the text.

2. *BIP* has multiple uses. If you know the author of a book, but aren't certain of the wording of the title, you might be able to verify it in the listing under the author. If you know the exact title but not the author, you can learn the name through the title index. Complete bibliographic data and the price are given. Paperback editions are included. When you have all the necessary information and wish to order the book, there is a directory of publishers in volume 7.

3. If a patron is interested in having a list of E. B. White's books that are available today, look in volume 3 (or, if using microfiche, in the alphabetical order under White). The authors' names are provided by their publishers or from their publishers' catalogs. You must check for all possible variant forms of names. Authors are found under their last names, followed by initials and first names; under true names; and under pseudonyms, some of which do not have cross-references.

   Look under Samuel Langhorne Clemens. There are entries for Clemens, S. L.; Samuel; Samuel L.; and Samuel Langhorne. There are *see* references to Twain, Mark, pseud. Spot-check similar listings of authors with pseudonyms.

4. *Books in Print* is available on microfiche, and is widely used in this form. The listings include forthcoming books and titles out-of-print. CD-ROM and online access to the databases of *Books in Print* are also available.

SUBJECT GUIDE TO BOOKS IN PRINT, 1957–
N.Y., R. R. Bowker, 1957– . 4v. Annual.

The *Subject Guide* is part of the triangle of R. R. Bowker titles listing books in current publication. It provides a subject analysis of the books included in the *Publishers' Trade List Annual* (q.v.) and *Books in Print* (q.v.).

This work is helpful, not only in assisting patrons, but also in selecting books for your library's collection. In the 1987–88 edition, the publisher states that there are more than 646,000 titles listed under 65,096 Library of Congress subject headings, with over 54,000 cross references! Each entry provides full bibliographic data. There is a directory of publishers and distributors with their addresses and phone numbers.

1. Read the section in the front of volume 1 entitled "How to Use the Subject Guide." Note the rules for subject arrangement.

2. Select a category that has a broad field of interest, such as music. From this general heading, look at the multiple subdivisions and cross-references. Repeat the process with oceanography, ecology, or a subject of your choice.

   To learn what biographical or critical works are available, look up a famous person of the past or present, such as Thomas Jefferson, Martin Luther King, Jr., Walt Whitman, a current head of state, or a contemporary author.

3. If a patron is disappointed because your library does not have a certain title, or needs titles on a subject of interest in addition to those you have cataloged, you will find the *Subject Guide* a most useful source for alternative or additional titles.

4. *BIP* and the *Subject Guide* are updated by the bimonthly Bowker title *Forthcoming Books*.

Z
1215
U6

CUMULATIVE BOOK INDEX:
A World List of Books
in the English Language
N.Y., H. W. Wilson, 1898– . Monthly except August.

The *CBI* is an international, authoritative, and comprehensive bibliography of current books published in the English language. Foreign books, such as dictionaries and editions of foreign classics, are included if they contain some English. Notable exclusions, of which librarians must be cognizant, are government publications, pamphlets, those materials regarded by the publishers as ephemeral, and others listed in the prefatory note. It is published monthly, except August, with a bound annual cumulation.

The arrangement consists of a single alphabetical listing of author or editor, title, and subject entries. Additional entries for illustrator, translator, and coauthor are included when appropriate. Author, or "main," entries contain the most information for each book. They provide the full name (including pseudonyms), title, complete bibliographic information, price, and ISBN, and Library of Congress card number when available.

1. Look up a broad subject, such as medicine, labor, or terrorism. Notice the multiple *see also* and *see* references and subdivisions.

2. Even a brief examination of the *CBI* should indicate its value and use. However, it is also important to know when *not* to consult the *CBI*. If a patron wants to know who published Robert Frost's *Complete Poems* but does not know when it was published, it would be quicker to look in *Books in Print* (q.v.). Using the *CBI* for such a question usually means a long search because you must start with the latest issue and work back until you find the complete edition of Frost's poetry. If the desired book is still in print, you should find it quickly in the author volume of *BIP.* With experience, the librarian soon learns when to search the *CBI* and when to turn to *BIP.*

3. At the end of each volume, there is a directory of publishers and distributors.

Z
5916
W74

FICTION CATALOG, 11th ed.
Edited by Juliette Yaakov
N.Y., H. W. Wilson, 1986. viii, 951p.

The *Fiction Catalog* is published quinquennially with four annual supplements. It is considered a companion to the nonfiction *Public Library Catalog* (q.v.). Titles are selected with the assistance of librarians from various public library systems and include currently published novels, novelettes, short stories, composite works, large-type editions, and out-of-print titles, written in or translated into English.

The *Fiction Catalog* is arranged in three parts: part 1 lists the authors (or main entries) in alphabetical order, their selected titles with complete bibliographic information, and brief summaries of the works. Excerpts of reviews, with the sources cited, are provided for most titles. "Titles have been catalogued, with minor exceptions, under the author's name as it appeared on the title page. References have been made from known variations of the author's name" (Preface). Part 2 is a title and subject index to part 1, in a single alphabetical arrangement. Part 3 is a directory of publishers and distributors of the books listed.

The examples given below can be found in the eleventh edition.

1. Reference librarians are frequently asked to identify novels when a reader remembers only the author or title or subject. This can be quite a challenge if all that is remembered is "what it's about." For example: A reader saw a movie on television that was based on a novel. It was about prisoners of war in World War II and a man who betrayed and used the other prisoners, who called him "Rat."

   As you turn to the subject index of the *Fiction Catalog*, think of as many associated subjects as you can. There is no listing that applies under *Rat*—the subject is not about the rodent. If you search *prisoners of war, prisons and prisoners,* or *concentration camps,* after referring in part 1 to the summaries of the listed novels, you will not find the requested work. If you look under collaborationists, you will find a *see* reference to *World War II—collaborationists,* but still not your answer. There is a listing for prison camps with a *see* reference to *World War, 1939–1945—prisoners and prisons.* Among the novels cited is: Clavell, J. *King Rat.* In part 1 of the *Catalog,* in the entry for Clavell's novel, the summary of the plot matches the description given by the reader. You can easily learn from this the importance of subject associations and cross-references.

2. Look up Carlos Fuentes and Georges Simenon. Note that the information includes the language and dates of the original editions, the editions in English and names of the translators, whether the titles are out-of-print, or, if available, the prices, and ISBNs. Summaries of the works follow and, for many, excerpts of reviews with sources.

3. The *Fiction Catalog* lists collected short stories. If you were asked for the titles of collections by William Faulkner, you would find

several. (The short story titles under *The Faulkner Reader* and *The Portable Faulkner* are not identified as such, but there is the notation "Analyzed in Short story index." If the reader's inquiry was specifically for Faulkner's story "Crevasse," you would find it in the contents listed for *Collected Stories of William Faulkner* but not in the title index at the end of the *Catalog*. A better approach would be to refer to the *Short Story Index* (q.v.), which would list the story by author and title, and possibly cite additional sources.

4. It should be remembered that not all titles selected receive unqualified recommendations, as can be noted in the reviews chosen for Simone de Beauvoir and Joseph Heller; and not all popular authors are included.

5. The title and subject index includes such broad headings as *psychological novels*, *social problems*, and *satire*, as well as *mysteries*, *science fiction*, *Western stories*, etc.

Z
1035.1
G45

GENERAL REFERENCE BOOKS FOR ADULTS: Authoritative Evaluations of Encyclopedias, Atlases, and Dictionaries
Marion Sader, Editor
The Bowker Buying Guide Series. N.Y., R. R. Bowker, 1988. xvi, 614p.

General Reference Books for Adults provides for "some 215 encyclopedias, world atlases, dictionaries, word books, and large-print reference works ... systematic, clearly organized, comparative reviews that follow consistent criteria. To be included in this volume, a reference work had to be appropriate for the general reference collection and readily available in the United States as of April 1, 1988" (Preface).

At the beginning of the book, there is a list of titles reviewed, a roster of consultants, reviewers, and contributors, and a guide, "Using This Book."

1. The work is divided into five parts: "Introduction" (with chapters titled "The History of General Reference Books," "Choosing General Reference Books," "Librarians Rate General Reference Books," and "Comparative Charts"); "Encyclopedias," "Atlases," "Dictionaries and Word Books," and "Large-Print General Reference Books." Each section begins with an introduction on what

to look for in the respective forms and an explanation of the criteria used to evaluate the entries.

For each work, there is a box titled "Facts at a Glance," which gives complete bibliographic information, price, method of sale, and revision policy. Each review follows a standard format, including essential elements for consideration, with a summary evaluation.

2. In part 1 you will find interesting highlights on the history of general reference books, including Dr. Johnson's dictionary and Noah Webster's American dictionary. Chapter 2 has a section on consumer-protection laws relating to the purchase of encyclopedias; chapter 3 tabulates questions and answers from a national survey of librarians to rate particular encyclopedias, atlases, and dictionaries; and chapter 4 presents comparative charts that "provide basic factual information about every reference book or set evaluated in *General Reference Books for Adults*" (p. 35).

3. Turn to part 2, "Encyclopedias." The introductory chapter has helpful information and follows the subheadings used for the reviews. Select several encyclopedias (including one that you have not used) and read the analyses. Note the facsimiles of pages, as that from the *New Encyclopaedia Britannica* (q.v.); the comparisons made to different encyclopedias; and the inclusion of other opinions.

4. In the introductory chapter to atlases there are illustrations and definitions of types of maps, as political, physical, thematic, and projection, followed by a glossary of cartographic terms.

Were you aware that the same cartography is used in different atlases published by one or more publishers? See the entries for the *New International Atlas* (Rand McNally) and the *International World Atlas* (Hammond). In the reviews of the atlases, the uniform attention given to criteria for evaluation provides an assurance of objectivity.

5. For dictionaries, in part 4, an outline of the structure of reviews is given on page 229, followed by tables comparing phonetic alphabets and a glossary of terms relating to dictionaries. For selected works there are facsimiles of entries with margin notes explaining special features. Sample entries also appear in the text. Separate similar coverage is given to etymological dictionaries, thesauri, and other word books. Do you find the seemingly endless use of

"Webster's" in the titles confusing? Remember the section in part 1 on Noah Webster's American dictionary (p. 11).

Part 5 provides analyses of large-print general reference books.

6. At the end of the book there is a bibliography, list of publishers, acknowledgments, and an index.

Z
1037.1
R43

REFERENCE BOOKS FOR YOUNG READERS: Authoritative Evaluations of Encyclopedias, Atlases, and Dictionaries
Marion Sader, Editor
The Bowker Buying Guide Series. N.Y., R. R. Bowker, 1988. xii, 615p.

"This guide, *Reference Books for Young Readers,* is designed primarily for those librarians who serve children and young adults—from preschool and kindergarten through elementary, middle school, and high school—in a reference capacity. . . . It presents approximately 200 extensive, descriptive evaluations of encyclopedias (online as well as printed versions), world atlases, dictionaries and word books, and large-print reference works . . . published in the United States . . . in print and readily available for purchase on August 1, 1987" (Preface).

The five-part division of this work and the uniform format of the entries are the same as found in *General Reference Books for Adults,* described in detail in the entry above.

1. Read the preface, in which you will find the editor's recommendation to "read the introductory, 'Using This Book,' which serves as a road map to the main features of the guide and describes the structure of this volume."

2. Many of the entries appear in *General Reference Books for Adults,* with, of course, the exceptions of those published specifically for children and young adults, as the *Merit Students Encyclopedia,* the *Rand McNally Children's Atlas of the World,* and the *American Heritage Student's Dictionary.* Read the entries for these and the entries listed for comparison.

   Note the facsimiles of pages from the works evaluated, as that from *Compton's Encyclopedia* (Chicago, Encyclopaedia Britannica, 1987), and from the *Macmillan First Dictionary* (N.Y., Macmillan, 1987).

3. Two appendixes contain a select bibliography and a list of publishers, followed by acknowledgments and an index.

"*Reference Books for Young Readers* presents the most extensive, methodical reviews of all three categories of general reference books that have yet been compiled into one comprehensive volume" (p. viii).

SELECTED INTRODUCTORY GUIDES
TO GOVERNMENT PUBLICATIONS

The U.S. government conducts one of the largest publishing offices in the world. Its publications cover the vital statistics and many interests of our lives, as well as the activities of the government in all its branches. These publications are for the most part incredibly inexpensive; nowhere else can one get so much quality for so little money. Although the term *government* encompasses municipal, state, and federal governments, emphasis is generally placed on those issued by the federal government.

Where can the reference librarian get information about government publications? In addition to sources described in these chapters, the following titles are useful for information on selection and the important nationwide system of depository libraries for government publications.

Guide to Popular U.S. Government Publications. Compiled by LeRoy C. Schwarzkopf. Littleton, Colo., Libraries Unlimited, 1986.

Introduction to United States Public Documents, 3d ed. By Joe Morehead. Littleton, Colo., Libraries Unlimited, 1983.

Using Government Publications. By Jean L. Sears and Marilyn K. Moody. Phoenix, Oryx Press, 1985–86. 2v.

Z
1223
Z7G68

GOVERNMENT REFERENCE BOOKS:
A Biennial Guide to U.S. Government
Publications, 1968/69–

Englewood, Colo., Libraries Unlimited, 1970–   .

Government Reference Books is an annotated guide to atlases, bibliographies, catalogs, compendia, dictionaries, directories, and other reference works issued by agencies of the U.S. government in a two-year period. Annotations are "descriptive, rather than critical, of purpose and contents. No attempt has been made to evaluate the usefulness of the publications" (Introduction).

The entries are organized by subject under four broad categories: General Library Reference; Social Sciences; Science and Technology; and Arts and Humanities. Complete bibliographic information is given whenever available, as well as the ISBN, Superintendent of Documents classification and stock numbers, Library of Congress classification and card number, and price.

1. Look through the table of contents for an overview of the subjects and arrangement of the book. Read the section titled "Compiler's Information," which explains the entries.

2. In the 1986/87 edition, compiled by LeRoy C. Schwarzkopf, turn to the section "Area Studies and Geography, General Works." The first entries are for the series *Area Handbooks* of the Department of the Army, followed by *Background Notes* issued by the Department of State. These are very useful publications on countries of the world. Read the annotations and scan the names of countries included. Decode the information given in several of the entries.

3. Choose subjects of interest, such as visual and performing arts; health sciences, medical care and treatment; immigration; and law, to learn what is available.

The index is by author, title, and subject. There is now a companion volume, *Government Reference Serials*, compiled by LeRoy C. Schwarzkopf (Englewood, Colo., Libraries Unlimited, 1988).

Z
1033
M5G8

GUIDE TO MICROFORMS IN PRINT: AUTHOR-TITLE. Incorporating International Microforms in Print, 1977–
Westport, Conn., Meckler. Annual.

The *Guide* is generally considered the equivalent of *Books in Print* for microforms. It "is a cumulative annual listing of microform titles, comprising books, journals, newspapers, government publications, archival material, collections, and other projects, etc., which are currently available from micropublishing organizations throughout the world" (Introduction). The entries are in alphabetical arrangement by author-title, and include author, title, volume, date, price, publisher, and type of microform. Cross-references are provided.

The introduction is printed in English, French, German, and Spanish, followed by one directory of publishers in alphabetical order and a second in code order.

1. Read the introduction, which gives a clear explanation of the entries, including the price code and microform designations.

2. If a library patron wishes to know if the works of H. H. Bancroft, the famous authority on the history of California, are available on microform, you would find the entry:

    Bancroft, Hubert Howe. WORKS. San Francisco,
          1882–90. 39v. 585.00; DA; 1.

    The titles in the *Guide* are in all capital letters. The date of the work is that of the publication in its original form. The number of volumes and price are followed by the publisher code (DA for Datamics, Inc.) and the code for the type of microform (1: reel microfilm; 35 mm.). Another entry for the Bancroft work lists *apply* in place of the price. What does that indicate? The publisher code is "AMU;5." Look up the name and address of the firm in the directory of publishers listed by codes.

3. Is the *Library Journal* available on microform? Can a complete set be obtained?

4. There is a companion publication, *Subject Guide to Microforms in Print* (1978–) with the same international coverage.

Z	**GUIDE TO REFERENCE BOOKS, 10th ed.**
1035	**Edited by Eugene P. Sheehy**
W79	Chicago, American Library Association,
	1986. xiv, 1,560p.

The *Guide to Reference Books* is a definitive, comprehensive work, worldwide in scope, explicit in style, and meticulously accurate in detail. In this tenth edition, over 14,000 international reference sources are annotated.

The first edition, edited by Alice Bertha Kroeger and published by the American Library Association in 1902, marked the beginning of what was to become a library tradition. Its early success as a text for the training of librarians led to annual supplements and a revised edition in 1908. After Kroeger's death in 1909, Isadore Gilbert Mudge undertook the continuation of the *Guide*. From that time, "the Reference Department of the Columbia University Libraries has been the work's home base" (p. ix). Over a period of thirty years, Mudge compiled the third through the sixth editions. She received international recognition from librarians for her bibliographical achievement and her role in raising the standards of reference collections and upgrading the work of reference librarians. When she retired in 1941, the American Library Association asked Constance Winchell to carry on the work, which, by this time, had become a classic tool for librarians. Winchell prepared supplements to the sixth edition, and in 1951 she edited the much enlarged seventh edition. This led to her monumental contribution to bibliographic resources, the eighth edition, in 1967. Since Winchell's retirement, Eugene P. Sheehy has continued this tradition of excellence in the ninth and tenth editions.

Viewed by beginning library and information science students, the *Guide* is awesome indeed, but initiated students and experienced librarians find it a most useful and indispensable aid for reference service and collection development. The entries include complete bibliographical information; historical facts relating to the publication when appropriate; notes or annotations, sometimes in the form of a quotation from the author, publisher, or a review; and, for most, the Library of Congress call number.

1. The arrangement is unique but practical. Each entry has its own code identification made up of letters and numbers.

   Look at the contents pages to see the plan of the main headings and subheadings. Not all the subheadings are listed in the contents. To find a specific work, you must use the index.

   The entries are divided into five major sections: "General Reference Works," "The Humanities," "Social and Behavioral Sciences," "History and Area Studies," and "Science, Technology, and Medicine."

   "In general, geographical arrangement within the sections follows the pattern: (1) International; (2) United States; (3) other countries in alphabetical order" (p. v).

2. Turn to the subdivision "Librarianship and Library Resources, AB." Scan the entries. Note the countries included and the forms of reference sources.

   Under the heading "Encyclopedias, AC," there is an introduction to the evaluation of encyclopedias with a detailed outline of what factors should be considered. You will find these helpful introductions before major sections and subdivisions, as "Science, Technology, and Medicine," "Government Publications," "Humanities," and "Theater and Performing Arts."

   Choose a section and look carefully at the scope of coverage, as

"Race Relations and Minorities" (p. 700); "National Politics and Government" (p. 854); and "Literature" (p. 406).

3. The editor states in the preface that, when an effort was made to provide a section on databases, "it was quickly apparent that this was an area of such rapid change and expansion that it could not be dealt with adequately in a work of this kind. Neither, of course, could we totally ignore the world of computerized database searching" (p. x). Coverage was limited to a few standard guides and directories, and the indication in the entries for hard-copy bibliographic tools "that *some portion* of the published bibliography, index, or other source is available for online searching. Thus, a black bullet (●) following the Library of Congress class mark serves to indicate some online availability, but it does not necessarily mean that the whole file of the publication is searchable online" (p. x).

4. At the beginning of the index there is an explanation of the entries. For an appreciation of the Index, see the listings *bibliographie, bibliography* and *biography.*

Z
6941
K2

MAGAZINES FOR LIBRARIES:
For the General Reader and School,
Junior College, College, University,
and Public Libraries, 5th ed.
By Bill Katz and Linda Sternberg Katz
N.Y., R. R. Bowker, 1986. xvii, 1,057p.

This annotated listing of periodicals by subject represents "what the editors and consultants believe to be the best and most useful for the average primary or secondary school, public, academic, or special library. . . . Annotations are intended to show purpose, scope, and audience for the periodicals, and most of them reflect some value judgment" (Preface). Read the preface, which explains the selection policy and the contribution of the consultants.

Study the section "How to Use This Book." There is an example of the bibliographic form of the entries, with explanations where considered necessary. This is followed by lists of abbreviations used in the text, consultants identified by initials, and microform and reprint companies.

"The periodicals in this book are listed alphabetically, by title, under the subjects given in the Contents. . . . The reader should refer to the index when a title is not found under the first subject consulted" (p. xi). *See also* references are provided under headings where considered necessary or helpful.

"Each magazine has an indication of audience or type of library for which it is suited. The scale is specific, but as most magazines are for more than one audience, several audience levels are usually given for each title" (p. xii). The key to abbreviations used to indicate the audience is under "General Abbreviations" (p. xiii).

Major subject indexes to the periodicals are cited, but for some titles not all indexing is included.

1. Refer to the table of contents for the comprehensive listing of diverse subjects, then look through the first section, "Abstracts and Indexes," for an overview of what is available.

    Turn to the subject *medicine and health.* The subdivisions for the section are listed, with *see also* references to other subjects in the work. The name and address of each contributor is given. There is a brief introduction to the periodicals of the field, a list of basic periodicals, and basic abstracts and indexes. The subjects range widely: health industry, health professions, public health, medicine-professional, and medicine and society.

    Under *medicine-professional,* find the title *JAMA: the Journal of the American Medical Association,* and interpret each item of the entry. Note the designated audience. How does this compare with the *New England Journal of Medicine?*

2. The section on newspapers of the United States provides excellent capsuled information. Newspapers and periodicals are also listed by region, as under *Europe, U.S.S.R.,* and *Eastern Europe.*

3. There is a subject-title index with *see* and *see also* references.

Z
6945
M33

MAGAZINES FOR SCHOOL LIBRARIES:
For Elementary, Junior High School,
and High School Libraries
By Bill Katz
N.Y., R. R. Bowker, 1987. xvii, 238p.

Magazines for School Libraries "meets a need for a selection of titles geared specifically to children, teenagers, and those professionals dealing with these groups" (Preface). This work is patterned after the editor's *Magazines for Libraries* (q.v.). Titles were selected and "with minor editing, annotations are taken directly from the fifth edition of *Magazines for Libraries*. Some additional titles, often new magazines, have been added" (p. vii).

The introduction presents the criteria for the selection of titles, methods of evaluating magazines, and sources of reviews, and cites comprehensive guides and basic manuals on acquiring, organizing, and managing periodical collections.

"The periodicals in this book are listed alphabetically, by title, under the subjects given in the Contents" (p. xiii). Subject listings are divided by designation of the intended readers, as for students and for professionals. The annotation for each periodical ends with an audience designation of elementary-junior high school, high school, or professional.

Refer to the article on *Magazines for Libraries* in this chapter for an explanation of the format and coverage presented in these related works.

MONTHLY CATALOG OF UNITED STATES GOVERNMENT PUBLICATIONS. 1895–
Washington, D.C., Superintendent of Documents,
U.S. Government Printing Office, 1895–   . Monthly.

The *Monthly Catalog* lists publications issued by all branches of the government. However, it is not a listing of all publications put out by the various agencies. The *Catalog* consists of the text and indexes by author, title, subject, series/report number, contract and stock numbers, and a title keyword.

In the front of the issues there is a users' guide, information on sales, order forms, and the Federal Depository Library Program, and a list of government authors.

1. In the beginning of the volume find the sample entry which provides a concise explanation of each part of an entry.

2. If you were looking for a publication on juvenile courts in the January, 1989, issue, you would find that heading in the subject index. One entry is listed as 89-3020 (the first two numbers stand for the year). Turn to the main section, where the entry number is listed in numerical order. The author of the publication is Howard N. Snyder. The title is *Court Careers of Juvenile Offenders*. Note the detailed cataloging. If any of the information cited is not

clear to you, refer again to the sample entry at the front of the volume.

3. Remember that the indexes are essential to the efficient use of this *Catalog.*

Z
881
A1U372

NATIONAL UNION CATALOG
Washington, D.C., Library of Congress.

"The *National Union Catalog* represents the works catalogued by the Library of Congress and by the libraries contributing to its cooperative cataloging program during the period of its coverage. In addition, it includes entries for monographic publications issued in 1956 and thereafter reported by . . . [cooperating] . . . North American libraries and not represented by LC printed cards. It constitutes a reference and research tool for a large part of the world's production of significant books as acquired and catalogued by the Library of Congress and a number of other North American libraries.

"For monographic works published since 1956 this catalog indicates at least one library where the publication is held and serves thereby, at least for those imprints, as a National Union Catalog. . . . [It] contains currently issued Library of Congress printed card entries for books, pamphlets, maps, atlases, periodicals and other serials, regardless of imprint date" (Foreword). The Library of Congress entries include works published in most of the world's languages.

Entries for music and musical sound recordings appear in the supplementary catalog, *Music, Books on Music and Sound Recordings*, although librettos, books about music and musicians, and nonmusical sound recordings are included in both catalogs. All LC entries for motion pictures and filmstrips are listed in another supplementary catalog, *Audiovisual Materials.*

In the development of the *National Union Catalog* there were several changes in the title, content, and form from its beginning in 1942 to 1982. The most radical change was made in 1983, when the Library of Congress began publishing it in microfiche only.

1. Read the foreword in a current cumulation, which gives the history of the *NUC* and the titles of additional LC catalogs, such as the *Register of Additional Locations* and the *National Register of Microform Masters.* There is an explanation of entries and of the LC

printed cards. This is followed by a description of the elements of the entries and symbols of participating libraries.

2. There is perhaps no better guide to the works of a world-famous author than the *National Union Catalog*. As evidence of this, see the entries for Dante Alighieri in the initial edition of the *Catalog*, which was titled the *Catalog of Books Represented by the Library of Congress Printed Cards Issued to July 31, 1942* (now incorporated in: *National Union Catalog, Pre-1956 Imprints. A Cumulative Author List* . . . [London], Mansell, 1968–1980.) The order of arrangement follows a general pattern for all the great and prolific writers in world literature: manuscripts, complete and selected works, individual works, and translated titles. Notice that for Dante, titles in Italian are listed first, bilingual titles are second, and titles in alphabetical order by language follow. Remember that these entries are for the period ending in 1942! Here is an exciting opportunity to learn the scope and gain an appreciation of an author's accomplishment.

3. The *National Union Catalog* microfiche editions are published in an index/register arrangement. The indexes—name, title, subject, and series—are the access points to the registers. A bibliographic record is located by searching an *NUC* index. Index entries, arranged alphabetically, are briefer than the register records, but may provide sufficient bibliographic information to end a search. The complete bibliographic record is listed in the *NUC Books Register*, which is arranged sequentially in register number order.

   There are also the *NUC Audiovisual Materials Index* and *Register*; and the *NUC Cartographic Materials Index* and *Register*.

   The *Register of Additional Locations* (*RAL*) provides the location of monographic titles cited in the *NUC*. The entries are arranged in order of the Library of Congress Card Number.

4. In a current microfiche edition:
   a. Look up, in *NUC Books*, William Faulkner to see the multiple languages into which Faulkner's works have been translated; note that the original English titles are given.
   b. Locate *United States. Office of Nuclear Regulatory Research* for an example of what information can be obtained from the detailed descriptive cataloging provided.
   c. Use the alphabetical *subject index* to find listings under *aeronautics* or *drug abuse*, as well as a broad subject of choice or one that you have researched previously without using the

NUC. There are many subdivisions and cross-references to assist in a search for a specific topic. The *Library of Congress Subject Catalog* was first issued in 1950, and is a remarkable, unique and important bibliography.

If you have not used the source *Library of Congress Subject Headings,* 10th ed. (Washington, D.C., 1986), which gives the subject headings established and used by the library, you should read the front matter and look through the listings of the current edition.

d. To learn to locate the names of libraries that might have a needed publication available for interlibrary loan, look it up in the January–December 1987 *NUC Books.* Name index:

Caughey, John Walton
California's own history . . . Sacramento,
California, State Department of Education,
1965.
NUC 87-12613   b-490-467

The number at the bottom of the entry, 87-12613, is the Library of Congress card number. Refer to the *NUC Register of Additional Locations* in which the entries are arranged in order of LC card number. The location symbol for the book is CU-BANC. In the section "Symbols of Participating Libraries," the library is identified as the University of California, Berkeley, Bancroft Library, with the city, state, and zip code.

The number at the right margin of the entry, b-490-467, is the register number, under which the book would be listed in the *NUC Books Register.*

The contribution and importance of the *National Union Catalog* are well described in the *Guide to Reference Books,* edited by Eugene P. Sheehy (q.v.): "Because of the immensity of the collections, the excellence of the cataloging, and the full bibliographical descriptions, the *Catalog* of the Library of Congress has been for many years an invaluable work in any library and indispensable in those where research is done" (p. 12). There is no bibliographical source comparable to the *NUC.*

Z
1215
P97

PUBLISHERS' TRADE LIST ANNUAL, 1873–
N.Y., R. R. Bowker, 1873–   .

The *PTLA* is a compilation of specially produced publishers' catalogs bound together in alphabetical order. Each catalog is inserted as it was issued by the publisher. Bowker does not rearrange or edit the data. The listings now include products of micropublishers and database publishers.

In the front of the first volume there is a section of yellow pages to accommodate the listings of small or specialty presses, and those publishers who do not want to supply printed catalogs in quantity. The yellow-page section also includes three indexes. The index to publishers cites every publisher represented in the *PTLA* with the address and the ISBN prefix. A page number following the publisher's name indicates that the information is in the yellow pages; an asterisk following the name indicates that the publisher has a catalog insertion. Next is the subject index to publishers, which identifies the major subject specialties of each house. The third index is to publishers' series, which is an alphabetical listing by series name.

1. In the preface, read the sections on the organization and uses of *PTLA*.

2. Through the index to publishers, locate the Country Music Foundation Press. What type of books does the press publish?

3. Turn to the subject index to publishers. What are the names of some reprint firms? How many publishers are producing books on women's studies?

4. Changes in the publishing field can be noted in the index to publishers. Check the entries for T. Y. Crowell and Funk & Wagnalls.

5. What is the name and address of the publisher of the series *Crosscurrents/Modern Critiques*?

6. Leaf through a volume to see the great differences in format, content, and print of the various catalogs.

Z
1035.1
R435

RECOMMENDED REFERENCE BOOKS FOR SMALL AND MEDIUM-SIZED LIBRARIES AND MEDIA CENTERS
Bohdan S. Wynar, Editor
Englewood, Colo., Libraries Unlimited, 1981– .

The reference books reviewed are selected from the *American Reference Books Annual* (q.v.). The editor states in the introduction (1988) that "since *ARBA* provides comprehensive coverage of all reference books, not just selected or recommended titles, many of which are of interest only to large academic and public libraries, we felt the need to offer an 'abridged' version of *ARBA* especially for smaller libraries of all types. . . . Although this is a selection of 'recommended titles,' critical comments appearing in the original *ARBA* reviews have been retained in this volume."

1. Look through the contents pages to learn the scope and format. Note the long list of contributors following the introduction.

   There are four major parts: General Reference Works (arranged alphabetically, subdivided by form); followed by Social Sciences, Humanities, and Science and Technology (in which the chapters, arranged alphabetically, are organized by topic). Reviews are written by subject specialists and signed.

2. Choose several topics and read the reviews for the titles included, as ethnic studies and anthropology, national literature, and decorative arts. There are additional reviews cited for many of these works.

Z
1035.1
A47

REFERENCE SOURCES FOR SMALL AND MEDIUM-SIZED LIBRARIES, 4th ed.
Compiled by the Ad Hoc Committee for the Fourth Edition, Reference and Adult Services Division, American Library Association
Jovian P. Lang and Deborah C. Masters, Coeditors and Chairpersons
Chicago, American Library Association, 1984.
xvi, 252p.

The scope of this book in the fourth edition "was expanded to include reference materials for children and young adults as well as adults; sources in other formats such as microforms and databases were added, and out-of-print sources considered to be basic reference sources were included" (Preface). It is intended for use in public, college, and large secondary school libraries. The criteria for the selection of titles are explained in the preface.

Complete bibliographic information is given for each source, including price, ISBN or ISSN, and microform/online availability, followed by an annotation. At the end of some of the annotations, on the right margin, the letters "J" and "Y" indicate the material could be useful for children (juvenile) or young adults.

The chapters of the book are arranged in the order of the Dewey

Decimal Classification. The names of the contributors for each chapter are shown under the chapter heading. The index at the back of the book is by author and title. The numbers refer to the entries, not to pages.

1. The contents pages detail the subjects and subdivisions of each section. Look through the headings under science and technology, then turn to that chapter for the multiple annotated entries, beginning with general: bibliographies and indexes, biographical sources, directories, encyclopedias, dictionaries, and handbooks to the specific subjects of the field, from aeronautics and space science to zoology.

   See how this format and coverage are repeated for other subject areas. This work can be useful also in book selection, as in the listing in the chapter on language of foreign-language dictionaries, and as a checklist for small libraries planning to expand their reference collections.

Z
1223
Z7J32

SUBJECT GUIDE TO MAJOR UNITED STATES GOVERNMENT PUBLICATIONS, 2d ed.
By Wiley J. Williams
Revised and expanded. Chicago, American Library
Association, 1987. xi, 257p.

The intent and scope of this *Subject Guide* are described in the preface, in which the author reminds us that "the body of publications of the federal government is huge, varied, and often complex. From this mass, this guide selectively attempts to identify some of the publications of permanent importance. This work is intended primarily for documents and reference librarians and for library or information science students. . . . [It] interprets "government publications" to mean "government *information* resources" regardless of format (books, pamphlets, periodicals, databases, microforms, archival/manuscript records, audiovisual materials, etc. . . . Items listed in this guide range from the earliest federal period to 1986; they were chosen with an eye toward their enduring significance" (Preface, p. viii–ix).

The text is arranged alphabetically by subject and has two appendixes. Each entry includes a full title, personal authors or editors (if any), date of publication, pagination, note of illustrations, series note (if applicable), issuing agency, and the Superintendent of Documents classification number.

1. After reading the preface, turn to the subject *courts*. What does the triangle symbol before the first paragraph indicate? There is a brief annotated bibliography of additional sources, including the names of online legal research systems. Cross-references are provided. Select several other subjects, such as medicine, natural resources, Afro-Americans, World War, 1939–45 (the early subject heading, European War, 1914–18 is used instead of World War I), and women. Remember that "United States" is omitted as the beginning of headings, presented as *history* or *navy*, instead of United States—History or U.S. Navy.

2. Appendix 1 is a supplementary, selected, annotated bibliography of guides, catalogs, indexes, and directories issued by the government and other publishers. Appendix 2 lists the Government Printing Office's *Subject Bibliographies* in numerical order. You will find references to these "SB" numbers throughout the text.

Z
692
V52V5

VIDEO FOR LIBRARIES: Special Interest Video for Small and Medium-Sized Public Libraries
Edited by Sally Mason and James Scholtz
Chicago, American Library Association, 1988. xxii, 161p.

In the introduction, the editors state that they "are proud to present this first comprehensive list of recommended videos for public libraries. . . . We have brought together a group of contributing editors with a wide range of expertise within the field of video in public libraries. We have called upon two of the major review sources in the field, *Booklist* and *The Video Librarian*. . . . *Booklist*'s criteria for selecting the films and videos were used" (p. ix).

1. Read the introduction, which provides an explanation of the entries.
    The classified entries are preceded by a section by James L. Limbacher on feature films on video in public libraries, listing videotape guides and recommended feature films in various categories.
    The text is arranged under the Dewey classification, adapted by the editors to fit the needs of this listing, with Library of Congress

subject headings. Each entry is annotated. The title, producer, date, time required, and price are included, with a classification number and subject heading. In the right margin the symbol "YA" indicates titles of special interest to young adults.

Look through the table of contents and select one or more subject areas, then read the entries. Note that, for many, as under *The Arts*, the names of the narrators or performers are given.

2. The children's list (p. 123–137) is in alphabetical order by title. "Titles chosen for the Association for Library Service to Children. *Notable Children's Films* list (1983–87) are indicated throughout" (p. 123).

3. The appendixes include titles of films for professional library viewing, addresses of producers/distributors, and video wholesalers and retailers.

There is a title index.

Reference should also be made to the annotated, cumulative listing *Notable Children's Films and Videos, Filmstrips, and Recordings, 1973–1986.* Prepared by Notable Films, Filmstrips and Recordings, 1973–1986 Retrospective Task Force, Association for Library Service to Children, American Library Association (Chicago, American Library Association, 1987).

A NOTE ABOUT RETROSPECTIVE BIBLIOGRAPHIES

In addition to maintaining current bibliographies of books currently now in print or recently out-of-print, such as *Books in Print* and the *Cumulative Book Index* (q.v.), large public, university, and special libraries acquire and retain retrospective bibliographies, which provide a historical record of what was published, where, and when (as in the United States, from 1639). Although our concern in this book is primarily with current bibliographies, you should be aware of noteworthy retrospective bibliographies. Many of the early national and international bibliographies have had supplements and indexes published, and some are now available on microform. For a comprehensive, annotated listing of retrospective bibliographies, refer to Sheehy's *Guide to Reference Books* (q.v.).

PERIODICALS

To keep this book within reasonable bounds, a limit has been placed on the listing of periodicals. Only selected titles generally considered essential sources for reviews of general reference works and on reference services are included. Periodicals published for the various specialties in library and information services, and those concerning audiovisual/nonprint materials or computer-assisted reference services, are now abundant and are cited with annotations in many of the works described or listed in these chapters. You should be aware of them and make an effort to look through issues to enlarge the scope of your professional knowledge.

Journals are the direction locators of today's professions. They make the difference between the dynamic and the static, the well-informed and the marginal librarian or information specialist. In library and information science schools, we are advised to read the journals "to keep up with the profession." When we have attained a satisfying position, we can all too easily believe that this is not necessary, with the exception of reading reviews. If you do not frequently read the articles in the journals cited in this section, and those for the various specialties in which you are interested, you may become like the proverbial ostrich. You might perform your work adequately, but you will neither fully appreciate the range or progression of the field nor realize your own potential.

Most of the periodicals listed here provide, in addition to reviews, information on areas such as reference techniques, book selection, online searching, audiovisual/nonprint materials, current issues, and projections for the field.

American Book Publishing Record. N.Y., R. R. Bowker, 1960– .
Monthly. Annual and five-year cumulations.
———, *Cumulative 1876–1949, 1980; Cumulative 1950–1977, 1979.*
On microfiche: *ABPR Index, 1876–1981, 1982.*
American Libraries. Chicago, American Library Association,
1907– . Monthly, except bimonthly July–August.
Booklist. Chicago, American Library Association, 1905– . 22/yr.
Choice. Chicago, American Library Association, 1964– . Monthly,
except combined July–August.
Library Journal. N.Y., R. R. Bowker, 1876– . Semimonthly; monthly
Jan., July, Aug., Dec.
Publisher's Weekly. N.Y., R. R. Bowker, 1872– . Weekly.

Reference Services Review: (R S R). Ann Arbor, Mich., Pierian Press, 1972– . Quarterly.

RQ. Chicago, American Library Association, 1960– . Quarterly.

School Library Journal. N.Y., R. R. Bowker, 1954– . Monthly, except combined June–July.

Top of the News. Chicago, American Library Association, 1942– . Quarterly.

VOYA: Voice of Youth Advocates. Virginia Beach, Va., VOYA, 1978– . Bimonthly.

Weekly Record. N.Y., R. R. Bowker, 1974– . Weekly

Wilson Library Bulletin. N.Y., H. W. Wilson, 1914– . Monthly, except July and August.

CHILDREN'S AND YOUNG ADULT SOURCES

Z
1037
L715

A TO ZOO: Subject Access to Children's Picture Books, 2d ed.
By Carolyn W. Lima
N.Y., R. R. Bowker, 1986. xx, 706p.

"Teachers, librarians, and parents are finding the picture book to be an important learning and entertainment tool. . . . The picture book, as broadly defined within the scope of this book, is a fiction or nonfiction title that has suitable vocabulary for preschool to grade two, with illustrations occupying as much or more space than the text" (Preface).

The guide is divided into five sections: Subject Headings, Subject Guide, Bibliographic Guide, Title Index, and Illustrator Index. Read the instructions in "How to Use This Book."

The introduction provides an interesting essay entitled "Genesis of the English-Language Picture Book," with a bibliography for additional reading.

1. The subject headings are arranged with subheadings in alphabetical order. These are followed by the subject guide, which lists the authors and titles of the picture books under the appropriate headings. See the titles under *behavior—sharing; birds* (with multiple subheadings, as *birds—owls*); *character traits—being different; folk and fairy tales;* and *Caldecott Award books.*

Parents frequently ask for picture books to help explain difficult subjects or experiences to their children, such as death, adoption, sibling rivalry, and hospitals. Look in the subject guide to learn what is available. There are also "wordless" books and books just for fun; see *toys—teddy bears* and *humor.*

2. The bibliographic guide is in alphabetical order by author (or title when the author is not known). Complete bibliographic data is given for each entry cited in the subject guide, with the subjects. The title and illustrator indexes complete the work. Note that, in the illustrator index, the name in parenthesis following the title is that of the author, as: Tudor, Tasha. The night before Christmas (Moore, Clement C.).

   The thorough indexing of the contents makes possible maximum use of this very helpful guide.

Z 1037 G48	**BEST BOOKS FOR CHILDREN: PRESCHOOL** **THROUGH THE MIDDLE GRADES, 3d ed.** **Edited by John T. Gillespie and Christine B. Gilbert** N.Y., R. R. Bowker, 1985. xii, 595p.

"As with the earlier editions, the primary aim of this work is to provide a list of books, gathered from a number of sources, that are highly recommended to satisfy both a child's recreational reading needs and the demands of a typical school curriculum. . . . For a title to be considered for listing, the basic requirement was multiple recommendations (usually three) in the sources consulted. . . . Beyond this, additional criteria included such obvious considerations as availability, up-to-dateness, accuracy, usefulness, and relevance" (Preface). Out-of-print titles and mass market series are not included.

The chosen titles are arranged "under broad interest areas, or, as in the case of nonfiction works, by curriculum-oriented subjects" (p. xii). In addition to bibliographic data, entries include grade levels, editions (as library binding or paperback), prices, awards received, other titles, and sequels and series by the author. Authors who are chiefly known by pseudonyms are not listed in the text nor in the index by their real names, as Dr. Seuss is not cross-referenced from Theodor Seuss Geisel, nor is Mark Twain from Samuel Langhorne Clemens.

There are four indexes: author/illustrator, title, biographical subjects, and subject. The numbers following each listing in the indexes refer to the entry numbers, not the page numbers.

1. For the best use of this comprehensive bibliography, look carefully through the detailed table of contents, which is arranged by subject headings and their subdivisions, including: preschool titles, fairy tales, fiction, multiple nonfiction/curriculum subjects, and biography.

2. Select several subjects and read the annotations of the works. Before recommending a book, the entire entry should be read. You can see the importance of this in the following two examples. The entry for Carol Brink's enduring story, *Caddie Woodlawn* (no. 2231), lists the publication date of 1973, which is for the edition cited. This is followed by the date of its Newbery Award, 1936. The titles under *federal government* (nos. 7365–7376), vary from a personal experience narrative to presidential trivia to studies of the structure of the government, with varying grade levels. The value of the annotations is apparent. In addition to the annotations, the editors provide recommendations for related works with the reference "also use." See entries no. 3309, a fantasy by Randall Jarrell, and no. 7099, a biography of Thomas Edison.

This bibliography is a valuable source not only for assisting children in selecting books, but also for preparing reading lists and for book selection.

CHILDREN'S BOOKS IN PRINT, 1969–
N.Y., R. R. Bowker, 1969–   . Annual.

This is a one-volume source for currently published children's books from preschool level to grade 12. In the 1987–88 edition, over 49,000 hardcover and paperback titles are listed. Grade levels are indicated. Sections are by author, title, and illustrator. Full bibliographic data is given. There is a directory of publishers and distributors with their addresses and phone numbers. Beginning with the nineteenth edition there is a listing of children's book awards.

SUBJECT GUIDE TO CHILDREN'S BOOKS IN PRINT, 1970–
N.Y., R. R. Bowker, 1970–   . Annual.

The *Children's BIP* is complemented by the *Subject Guide*. Books are listed under Sears and Library of Congress, subject headings.

A major difference between this work and the *Subject Guide* to the standard *BIP* is that the children's guide includes fiction and picture books. If a child asks for help with an assignment to read a story about dogs or some other animal of choice, you will find listings under the subjects. These fiction titles are, of course, in addition to the multiple nonfiction titles indexed by the subject.

FORTHCOMING CHILDREN'S BOOKS
N.Y., R. R. Bowker, 1988–   . Bimonthly.

Indexed by author, title, subject, and illustration.

Z
1037
C5443

CHILDREN'S CATALOG, 15th ed.
Edited by Richard H. Isaacson, Ferne E. Hillegas, and Juliette Yaakov
N.Y., H. W. Wilson, 1986. xiv, 1,298p.

"The first edition of *Children's Catalog* was published in 1909. From the beginning, the intent has been to include the best books for children in the fields of fiction and nonfiction . . . from pre-school through the sixth grade" (Preface). The bound edition is supplemented by four annual issues.

The *Catalog* is divided into three parts: the classified catalog; the author, title, subject, and analytical index; and the directory of publishers and distributors. It was compiled with the assistance of two advisory committees of librarians.

Read the short section "How to Use *Children's Catalog*," and note the outline of classification, as "Part 1 of the Catalog is arranged according to the Dewey schedules, and the outline thus serves as a table of contents" (p. xiv). The classification is from the *Abridged Dewey Decimal Classification*; the subject headings from the *Sears List of Subject Headings*.

1. In looking up entries for nonfiction, it is important to remember the editors' direction that "if a particular title is not found where it might be expected in the Classification, the Index in Part 2 should be checked to make certain the title is not classified elsewhere in the schedules" (p. x).

   If you wished to see if there is an entry for David Macaulay's book *Pyramid* and looked under the classification number for ancient Egypt, 932, you would not find it. The work is listed in the index under the author, title, and subject with the architecture classification of 726. For full bibliographic and cataloging information, price, ISBN, grade designation, and a summary and review, refer to the entry in part 1 under 726. Another work by this gifted author is under 728.8, *Castle*, with the notation, "A Caldecott Medal honor book, 1978."

2. The nonfiction is followed by fiction, story collections, and easy books. Read the explanations under the headings as to what is included in the "SC" and "E" sections.

   In addition to complete bibliographic data, entries for fiction titles include dates of first publication, editions available (as for Johanna Spyri and Louisa May Alcott), illustrators, translators, awards, summaries and reviews, and subject headings. Select some favorite authors or several at random to learn the format and content of the entries.

   Related works or titles in series are listed, as those by Walter Farley, Donald J. Sobol, Laura Ingalls Wilder, and C. S. Lewis. Fiction by subject can be found in the index, as represented in the lists for mysteries and detective stories, dogs, and U.S. history, by period.

3. Look through the easy books section, which provides the same detailed information as given for fiction.

   Remember that, with the exception of "modern" fairy tales (which are classed with fiction), fairy tales, fables, legends, and folk tales are classed in 398.2. See the entries for Paul Galdone, Howard Pyle, and Jacob Grimm. Where would you expect to find the works of Hans Christian Andersen?

4. The index, part 2, with authors, titles, subjects, and analytical entries, lists illustrators with the included titles of works illustrated (as those for N. C. Wyeth and Arlene Mosel); the contents of story collections, as for the *Rootabaga Stories* by Carl Sandburg and the fairy tale collection by Virginia Haviland; and multiple *see* and *see also* cross-references.

   As examples of reviews of an illustrator's contribution to children's books, look up in the Index and read the entries for Susan Jeffers.

5. The *Catalog* lists adult books, periodicals and review sources of

interest to children's librarians in the classifications of 011 through 028 and other subject areas.

6. Part 3 is a directory of publishers and distributors, with the full names and addresses of publishers cited in the entries.

Z
2014.5
S57

ELVA S. SMITH'S THE HISTORY OF CHILDREN'S LITERATURE: A Syllabus with Selected Bibliographies, revised and enlarged ed.
By Margaret Hodges and Susan Steinfirst
Chicago, American Library Association, 1980. 290p.

The preface to the revised edition and a restatement from the introduction to the first edition provide an understanding of the development of the book and the scope of the titles cited. The editors describe the first edition as a "landmark work" and advise that "nothing similar in form and substance has appeared" (Preface, p. viii). Coverage is from the sixth century to the close of the nineteenth and "limited to England and America except in cases where a foreign author was directly influential in the English or American development" (Preface, p. ix).

The latest date for titles in the book is 1977. This first revised edition includes most of the originally listed titles, with many additional works and a new section on folklore. Specific entries are easily located through the author-title index.

For each period of history, there is an introductory essay and an outline, followed by bibliographies of general references, educational background, individual writers (their works, translations, and illustrators, and biographical and critical works that appeared in both periodicals and books). Most of these are annotated.

There are extensive bibliographies on such long-popular children's authors as Louisa M. Alcott.

1. Look up a favorite author, but remember the inclusive dates of coverage described in the preface.
   Note that for classics originally written in a foreign language, the names of the first or early translators and the illustrators are listed.

2. An intriguing puzzle is the exclusion of Beatrix Potter from the author's section. She is included in the final chapter, entitled "Illustrators for Books for Children—Individual Illustrators."

In that same chapter, there are multiple entries for Howard Pyle dating from 1907 to 1977.

FANTASY LITERATURE FOR CHILDREN AND YOUNG ADULTS: An Annotated Bibliography, 3d ed.
By Ruth Nadelman Lynn
N.Y., R. R. Bowker, 1989. xlvii, 771p.

This annotated bibliography of fantasy novels and story collections is "for children and young adults in grades 2 through 12, as well as a research guide on the authors who write fantasy for children and young adults. The book is intended for use by librarians, teachers, parents, and students in children's and young adult literature courses" (Preface).

"The books in Part One, Annotated Bibliography, are novels and story collections published in English in the United States (including translations) between 1900 and 1988" (Preface). Selected nineteenth-century classics have been included. Reviews are cited in each entry, and only books recommended in two or more sources have been entered. Out-of-print titles are listed. Science fiction and horror literature are not included.

Grade levels are indicated in each entry, and, additionally, a grade level symbol appears in the left margin of each entry (C = grades 3–6; C/YA = grades 5–8; YA = grades 7–12). The listings include adult books that have become popular with young adult readers.

Selected titles have recommendation ratings placed in the left-hand margin: "[O], outstanding quality recommended in five or more professional review sources or generally regarded as "classics" by librarians who work with children and young adults, and [R], recommended in three to four review sources" (Preface).

Part 2, a research guide, presents bibliographies on reference and bibliography, history and criticism, teaching resources, and author studies.

1. Read the preface and the guide to use. These are followed by a listing of abbreviations used in the text. The introduction defines and discusses the purpose, categories, effect, and criticism of fantasy literature, and ends with a historical overview.

   The text begins with listings of outstanding contemporary

books and series. The complete bibliographic data and annotations will be found in the chapter entries.

2. Refer to the table of contents to learn what categories are used for the bibliographies. Note that there are indexes for authors and illustrators, titles, and subjects. The author index provides cross-references for pseudonyms.

3. Look up C. S. Lewis in the author index to locate the entry for his famous *Chronicles of Narnia*. The titles and dates of the individual books of the series are given, with brief annotations, the grade level and recommendation symbol for outstanding. The titles are cited in the order that the author wished them to be read—a very helpful consideration for librarians and readers. Review sources are given at the end of the annotations. The names of the illustrators for two editions are listed.

4. If you look in the title index for the *Pern* series by Anne McCaffrey you will not find it, but you will find it in the subject index. Look over the subjects, which include Native Americans; "King Arthur" adaptations; names of countries with subheadings for folklore, mythology, and historical periods and with a lengthy list under *United States*; and miniature people, with *see also* references to dwarfs, fairies, Lilliputians, etc.

5. In part 2, the research guide, note especially the chapter on author studies, which provides bibliographies of works by and about the authors represented in the text. As examples, see the entries for Natalie (Zane Moore) Babbitt, Kenneth Grahame, and Isaac Bashevis Singer.

Z
1037
W98

GUIDE TO REFERENCE BOOKS FOR SCHOOL MEDIA CENTERS, 3d ed.
By Christine Gehrt Wynar
Littleton, Colo., Libraries Unlimited, 1986. xv, 407p.

"This work is designed to be a comprehensive guide to current reference materials that are suitable for several categories of users: (1) students in elementary, middle, and high schools; (2) teachers K-12; (3) school library media specialists; and (4) educators in the areas of teacher preservice and inservice, information resources, and children's and young adult literature" (p. xi).

1. Read the introduction, which describes the development of the work, the criteria for selecting titles, and the use of the *Guide*.

   Look through the table of contents. Notice the listing of subjects from traditional to current concerns and interests.

2. There are fifty-four subject chapters arranged alphabetically, subdivided by form and/or topic. Full bibliographic data is given for each entry. Citations to reviews in selected major review sources are provided at the end of each entry. The entries are numbered in consecutive order. Those with the code "E" are for grades K-5; with "E+" suitable for grade 6 as well. No codes are used for grades 6 and up.

3. There is an author, title, and subject index, arranged in a single alphabet. Subjects are in boldface type.

4. Choose a section in the initial categories of media sources, media selection, or general reference and a specific subject chapter. Read the annotations of the works cited to gain an impression of the author's analysis and criticism in this detailed, comprehensive coverage.

Z
1039
S5

**HIGH INTEREST BOOKS FOR TEENS:
A Guide to Book Reviews and
Biographical Sources, 2d ed.**
Joyce Nakamura, Editor
Detroit, Gale Research, 1988. xxxvi, 539p.

"This is a tool for librarians, teachers in classrooms and reading laboratories, and others involved in guiding teens known to have learning disabilities or simply underdeveloped reading skills," which lists high-interest/low-readability level fiction and nonfiction for students in junior and senior high school, with review sources published in periodicals, and, for most, biographical sources for the authors (Introduction, p. vii).

"The Guide to Book Reviews and Biographical Sources, the main section of *High Interest Books for Teens*, is arranged alphabetically by author. Each entry gives the author's full name (or an identified pseudonym), dates of birth and death (if known), and one or more sources that give further biographical information" (Introduction, p. vii). Titles are not identified as fiction or nonfiction except in the subject headings at the end of the entries. Not all fiction titles have subject headings. At the back of the book there is a title index and a detailed subject index.

Read the introduction, which describes the work and provides sample entries. The introduction is followed by lists of the book reviews and biographical sources cited. Note the diversity of the periodicals and the biographical reference books cited, for which bibliographic information is given.

1. A very popular book among teenagers has been a biography of the football player Brian Piccolo. This is a good example of a motion picture and/or television movie creating interest in a book, and at the same time causing problems in associating the title of the film with that of the book. In this instance, the title frequently requested is *Brian's Song,* which the reader usually does not realize is a play. It is listed in the title index with the author's name, William Blinn. Under the author entry in the main section, there is a subject heading, *Piccolo, Brian—drama.* In the subject index, there is a listing for the play under Piccolo, but not for a biography. By turning to the subject, *football—biography,* you will find under Morris, Jeannie, the title *Brian Piccolo: A Short Season.* In the author entry for Jeannie Morris, nine reviews are cited. There are no biographical sources listed for the author, but sometimes enough information about an author can be obtained in reviews to satisfy a student's requirement.

2. Bibliographic information is not given for the books. This is a disadvantage in selecting and recommending nonfiction. A title under the subject *astronautics* is *American Women of the Space Age* by Mary Finch Hoyt. To obtain the publication date, you must refer to another source or consider the year the six reviews were published, which is 1966. For more current titles, there are three biographies of Sally Ride under *astronauts,* reviewed in 1983–85.

   As you will find in other reference book bibliographies, there is a mixture of possibly out-of-date titles with the current. *How To Be a Successful Teenager* was reviewed in 1967. Since the author was William C. Menninger, the editor might have retained it as a still valuable work. You can form your own evaluation by referring to the two reviews cited.

3. This guide can be helpful in assisting reluctant teenagers or those with learning disabilities with school assignments, especially through the subject index. The abbreviations used for the review

and biographical sources are fairly easy to decipher after initial
referrals to the keys at the front of the book (repeated on the front
and back endsheets).

Magazines for School Libraries; see *Magazines for Libraries* in this
chapter.

Reference Books for Young Readers; see *General Reference Books for
Adults* in this chapter.

SOFTWARE FOR SCHOOLS:
A Comprehensive Directory of Educational
Software, Grades Pre-K through 12
N.Y., R. R. Bowker, 1987. A-72, 1,085p.

"*Software for Schools* is a single, comprehensive guide to educational
microcomputer software from all publishers and distributors that is
suitable for use in a formal educational setting from preschool
through 12th grade. Unlike other software directories, *Software for
Schools* does not include software titles that are intended for use in
the home or as educational "entertainment." Although certain products may be suitable for both settings, the editors have chosen to
design this book for professional educators and librarians" (Preface).

The preface outlines the objectives and organization of the book.
At the beginning of the text, there are articles on the selection and
evaluation of software, the use and management of computers in the
classroom, and networking in schools.

1. The section "How to Use This Book" has explanations and sam-
   ples of entries. This is followed by a list of subject headings, checklists for software and hardware, and a helpful glossary.

2. The classroom software/grade level indexes list software packages
   for classroom use. The entries are by the name of the computer
   they will run on, then by subject with grade levels. The first page
   of the section gives an explanation of the content of the entries.
   The indexes begin with the Apple II family and compatibles. See
   the lengthy listings under *language arts—reading,* for grades PS–
   K through 10–12; *social sciences—U.S. history;* and *science—
   physics.*

3. The professional software indexes are for the interests of teachers
   and/or administrators. The contents of the entries are explained
   in the first page of the section.

4. The title index is the largest and most comprehensive section of the directory. It contains the entries of the two preceding indexes, listing the entries alphabetically by title, and provides more detailed information on each software package, including the author, grade levels, date, compatible hardware, operating system(s) required, language(s), memory required, other requirements, price and order number, and a descriptive annotation.

   Read the explanation of the entries given on the first page of the section. You might have to refer again to the example and instructions in the section "How to Use This Book."

   As examples, turn to the titles *Reader Rabbit; Music Theory—Advanced;* and *Tricky Spelling Checker.* The entries for novels are described as "works of literature" without credit to the authors, as *The Hobbit* and *Jane Eyre.* If you are not at ease with the technical data, you might appreciate the title entry *You Want Me to Teach What?*

5. The publishers index at the end of the book lists in alphabetical order the names of the software publishers represented, with addresses and phone numbers.

BIBLIOGRAPHIES

Additional Titles

Anatomy of Wonder: A Critical Guide to Science Fiction, 3d ed. Edited by Neil Barron. N.Y., R. R. Bowker, 1987.
Annotated bibliography by author under sections by historical period; children's and young adult science fiction; and American, English, and foreign-language titles. A chapter on research aids and a core collection checklist are provided. Many annotations for works by individual authors include "compare" and "contrast" titles by other authors.
The Best in Children's Books: The University of Chicago Guide to Children's Literature, 1979–1984. Written and edited by Zena Sutherland. Chicago, University of Chicago Press, 1986.
Reviews from the *Bulletin of the Center for Children's Books;* grade levels indicated.
Best Reference Books, 1981–1985: Titles of Lasting Value Selected from American Reference Books Annual. Edited by Bohdan S. Wynar. Englewood, Colo., Libraries Unlimited, 1986.

Books for Children to Read Alone: A Guide for Parents and Librarians. By George Wilson and Joyce Moss. N.Y., R. R. Bowker, 1988. Annotated; graded pre-K through grade 3.

Books for College Libraries: A Core Collection of 50,000 Titles, 3d ed. A Project of the Association of College and Research Libraries. Chicago, American Library Association, 1988. 5v.
Titles recommended to support undergraduate courses in all academic fields; very useful for bibliographic checking in subject areas for public libraries.

Books for the Gifted Child. V. 1 by Barbara H. Baskin and Karen H. Harris. N.Y., R. R. Bowker, 1980.
———. V. 2 by Gail A. Nelson and Paula Hauser. N.Y., R. R. Bowker, 1988.
Annotated, with designated reading levels, for preschool through grade 6.

Books in Series, 4th ed. N.Y., R. R. Bowker, 1985. 6v.
Comprehensive listing of titles and series arranged by Library of Congress headings, with author and title indexes cross-referenced to the main series index.

Children's Literature: A Guide to Reference Sources. Prepared under the Direction of Virginia Haviland. Washington, D.C., Library of Congress, 1966. Supplements, 1972; 1977.

First Readers: An Annotated Bibliography of Books for Children Beginning to Read. By Barbara Barstow and Judith Riggle. N.Y., R. R. Bowker, 1989.
Annotates "some 2,000" selected fiction and nonfiction titles for kindergarten through second grade. Indexed by subject, title, illustrator and reading level.

Genreflecting: A Guide to Reading Interests in Genre Fiction, 2d ed. By Betty Rosenberg. Littleton, Colo., Libraries Unlimited, 1986.

High-Low Handbook: Books, Materials, and Services for the Problem Reader, 2d ed. Compiled and edited by Ellen V. LiBretto. N.Y., R. R. Bowker, 1985.
Annotated bibliography of titles recommended for disabled or reluctant teenage readers. Reading/interest grade level indicated for each entry.

Junior High School Library Catalog, 5th ed. N.Y., H. W. Wilson, 1985.
With four annual paperbound supplements.

Monthly Checklist of State Publications. Washington, D.C., Library of Congress, 1910– .

Paperbound Books in Print. N.Y., R. R. Bowker, 1955– . Biannual.

Public Library Catalog, 8th ed. Edited by Gary L. Bogart and John Greenfieldt. N.Y., H. W. Wilson, 1984. With four annual paperbound supplements.

Reader's Adviser: A Layman's Guide to Literature, 13th ed. N.Y., R. R. Bowker, 1988. 6v.

A standard source of annotated bibliographies of "the best" titles in literature, art, social sciences, history, philosophy and religion, science, technology, and medicine; volume 6 provides name, title, and subject index to volumes 1–5.

Reference Books Bulletin. Chicago, American Library Association, 1970– . Annual.

Cumulation of *RBB* reviews published as part of *Booklist:* 22/yr. (Chicago, American Library Association, 1905–).

Reference Books for Children. By Carolyn Sue Peterson and Ann D. Fenton. Metuchen, N.J., Scarecrow Press, 1981.

Senior High School Library Catalog, 13th ed. N.Y., H. W. Wilson, 1987. With four annual paperbound supplements.

Sequences: An Annotated Guide to Children's Fiction in Series. By Susan Roman. Chicago, American Library Association, 1985.

Twentieth-Century Short Story Explication: Interpretations 1900–1975, of Short Fiction since 1800, 3d ed. By Warren S. Walker. Hamden, Conn., Shoe String Press, 1977.

———. Supplement, 1980.

The Video Source Book, 9th ed. Syossett, N.Y., National Video Clearinghouse, 1987. Distribution by Gale Research.

A World Bibliography of Bibliographies and of Bibliographical Catalogues, Calendars, Abstracts, Digests, Indexes, and the Like, 4th ed. By Theodore Besterman. Revised and greatly enlarged throughout. Lausanne, Societas Bibliographica, 1965–66. 5v.

An example of an extraordinary, comprehensive bibliography.

A World Bibliography of Bibliographies, 1964–1974: A List of Works Represented by Library of Congress Printed Catalog Cards. By Alice F. Toomey. Totowa, N.J., Rowman and Littlefield, 1977. 2v.

Published as a supplement to the fourth edition of Besterman, cited above.

7.

BIOGRAPHICAL SOURCES

People have an insatiable curiosity about other people, and the reference librarian is expected to have limitless access to biographical data on every named descendant of Adam and Eve. The person in question may be great or little known, living or dead, famous or infamous, an idol or a nonentity. Many a hero, having gloried for a long time in attention from a capricious public, is suddenly erased by the media. Such a forgotten figure is frequently an object of interest to a curious patron, who may wish to have a definitive biography or may simply need to verify a fact. Students continuously request information in capsule form about authors, or "whole books" on figures from antiquity or the current rock stars for a book report.

The catalog is, of course, the reference librarian's immediate aid. If no source is found, biographical information may be located in encyclopedias, collected biographies, history books, historical or critical works of a special field, periodicals, and newspapers, and through the use of special or general indexes, such as the *Biography Index* (q.v.).

In addition to the above materials, there are biographical dictionaries—the sources that this chapter is primarily concerned with. A biographical dictionary resembles a lexicon in that it is arranged alphabetically, gives the correct spelling of each name, and may show the correct pronunciation. Beyond the vital statistics, there is no limit to the kinds of information that may be included. Some biographical dictionaries cite only a few facts, whereas others devote many pages to each person and include critical or evaluative comment. Some of these append a bibliography of additional sources of information about the biographee. There are biographical dictionaries, universal in scope, that cover all periods of history, and others that limit their entries by place and time. There are those that include only people who have died, and others that include only the living. They may include or exclude mythological and legendary figures, exponents of a faith or philosophy, prominent figures in professions or the arts, women and/or men, well-known or little-known authors. As in all reference work, the fun and challenge is in the search, and the successful search is its own reward.

This chapter introduces you to some standard biographical sources. As a reference librarian, you must remember that biography means people, and information about people may be found in multiple, varied sources by librarians and information specialists with experience, thought, and persistence.

CT	**ALMANAC OF FAMOUS PEOPLE: A**
104	**Comprehensive Reference Guide to**
B56	**More Than 25,000 Famous and Infamous**
	Newsmakers from Biblical Times
	to the Present, 4th ed.
	Susan L. Stetler, Editor
	Detroit, Gale Research, 1989. 3v.

The *Almanac of Famous People,* formerly *Biography Almanac,* "is a biographical dictionary and an index to information about famous people. Fame has neither limitations nor definitions, standards nor rule. It thrives as a result of genius or eccentricity, accident or purpose" (Introduction, p. vii). The *Almanac* is a ready-reference source for identifying persons from all periods and throughout the world. The first two volumes of the three-volume work contain the biographical entries in alphabetical order; the third volume provides three indexes—chronological, geographical, and occupational.

Each entry gives the person's name (as most popularly known); where applicable, the pseudonym, real name, or group affiliation in brackets; nicknames in quotation marks; nationality; occupation; a one-line descriptor; date and place of birth and death, where applicable, and alphabetically arranged codes for additional biographical reference sources.

1. Read the introduction, which provides sample entries with explanations. This is followed by the key to abbreviations and the key to source codes. For the latter, note the extensive list of reference sources cited.

2. As examples of entries of nicknames and professional and religious names, look up General John J. Pershing, "Yogi" Berra, Bill Moyers, Mother Teresa, and Elizabeth Hanford Dole.

   Groups, as those in rock music and comedy acts, are listed with members cited in brackets. There is a main entry for each member, with the name of the group in brackets. See the *Beatles* and the *Marx Brothers*. There are also listings for groups or personalities joined by events, as *Stanley and Livingston* and *the hostages* (Americans captured in Iran in 1979).

3. The one-line descriptors tend to emphasize general, popular symbols of fame, which in some cases limit the understanding of the person's achievements, as Vladimir Horowitz appears to be known chiefly as the winner of fifteen Grammy Awards, and Marilyn Horne is recognized only as having dubbed the vocal score of a movie. However, other descriptors identify well the biographees' unique claims to fame, as do the entries for such differing careers and times as those for Eratosthenes, Erte, Harry Houdini, Casey Stengel, and Dame Nellie Melba.

4. As you read in the introduction (p. xii), cross-references are not provided for all names used by an individual. There is no *see* reference from Isak Dinesen to Karen Blixen; from St.-John Perse to Alexis St.-Leger Leger. There are *see* references from Clemens to Twain and from Famous Amos to Wally Amos.

5. The first index in volume 3 is the chronological index. It lists by month, day, and year the biographees who were born or who died on each date. Select a date and glance through the listing to be aware of the format. The second index, the geographical, is divided into three sections: the United States (by state and city), Canada (by province and city), and foreign (by country and city). Below each location are the names of the individuals, included in volumes 1 and 2, who were either born or who died in that location, with the birth or death dates. You will find Mozart listed under Salzburg, Austria, as his place of birth and under Vienna, Austria, as his place of death, with the dates. The number of worldwide locations is fascinating—from villages to suburbs to internationally famous cities. A place seeming as remote as Bloemfontein, South Africa, is cited as the birthplace of J. R. R. Tolkien; Summit, New Jersey, is the birthplace of Meryl Streep. Warm Springs, Georgia, is listed as the place of death of Franklin Delano Roosevelt, as Madrid, Spain, is for Bing Crosby. The occupational index is in alphabetical order by the occupations of the biographees from volumes 1 and 2. The headings include *abolitionists, aircraft manufacturers, celebrity relatives, reformers, Watergate participants,* to *zoologists.* However, the many activities listed do not eliminate

the need to search for related headings; cross-references are not provided. William O. Douglas is not under *judge*, but under *Supreme Court justice*. In that same list, Bertha Wilson is not identified as being on the Supreme Court of *Canada*, which could be misleading. Albert Bruce Sabin appears under *biologist*, not under *scientist*, as do others with more than one occupation. There is no heading for immunologist. This extensive index is very helpful to students and researchers. *See* and *see also* references should be added for more efficient and accurate use of the *Almanac*.

Z
5301
B5

BIOGRAPHY INDEX: A Cumulative Index to Biographical Material in Books and Magazines
N.Y., H. W. Wilson, 1947–   .

"The index is comprehensive in scope and is intended to serve general and scholarly reference needs. . . . All biographees are American unless otherwise indicated. . . . The main section of the index consists of index entries arranged alphabetically by the last name of the biographee. This is followed by a list of biographees organized by profession or occupation. A Checklist of Composite Books Analyzed is also included" (Prefatory Note).

The *Biography Index* is published quarterly, with annual and two-year cumulations. It is useful to the librarian as a checklist in book selection, in making bibliographies, and, most importantly, as a basic reference tool in locating biographical material on people from all periods of history and fields.

In the front of the volumes there is a sample entry and a key to abbreviations.

1. In the September 1986–August 1988 volume, turn to the entry for Martin Luther King, Jr. There is an extensive listing of biographies, collective biography, and periodical articles. Similar coverage is given the artist Georgia O'Keeffe.

   Is there an entry for Kiri Te Kanawa?

   If a young baseball buff wanted to know about Lou Gehrig, you would find an entry for the player, and under the subheading *juvenile literature*, a biography.

2. In the second section, the index to professions and occupations, the biographees are listed under their field of employment or ac-

tivity, as presidents (by country), basketball players, outlaws, dancers, journalists, etc. Notice the multiple *see also* references.

3. For the addresses of the book publishers cited in the entries, you are referred to the directory of publishers and distributors in the *Cumulative Book Index* (q.v.).

<table>
<tr><td>CT
103
C3</td><td>**CHAMBERS BIOGRAPHICAL DICTIONARY,
revised ed.**
J. O. Thorne and T. C. Collocott, Editors
Cambridge, Cambridge University Press, 1984. 1,493p.</td></tr>
</table>

The preface, written in a witty style, gives the background of this biographical dictionary and the changes made in the revised edition. "The unique position that *Chambers Biographical Dictionary* holds among works of its kind owes much to the policy of clothing the bare facts with human interest and critical observation, and in the new edition we have taken care to preserve this tradition" (Preface).

The biographees were chosen from all periods of history and fields of activity. Although there is some emphasis on those of British and European nationality, the scope is international.

1. To appreciate the style of writing and the coverage, read the articles on Dylan Thomas, Moshe Dayan, Richard Burton, Arturo Toscanini, and the Beatles.

    See the entries under *John* for the method of multiple listings of saints, popes, and kings. The omission of such internationally respected artists in music as Vladimir Horowitz, Isaac Stern, Itzhak Perlman may be questioned. Glenn Gould is included, as is Leonard Bernstein, but not Eugene Ormandy.

2. As an example of a listing of persons with the same surname, turn to the entry for *James*, where, following the entries for saints and kings, you will find the biographees alphabetically and numerically entered. Numbers (4) and (9) are on the famous brothers Henry and William. There are citations of books by and about them. This alphabetical/numerical arrangement of names is also used to distinguish among members of a family, as Roosevelt and Adams.

3. Do not overlook the subject index at the back of the book. Under the subject headings, related entries are listed, followed by the

names of biographees found in the text. Follow through on searches for information under the names of the persons listed under *exploration—Everest, literature—When We Were Very Young, music—Rhapsody on a Theme of Paganini,* and *science and industry—antibodies.* This is a ready-reference source to be remembered!

Z
1224
C6

CONTEMPORARY AUTHORS:
A Bio-Bibliographical Guide
to Current Writers
Detroit, Gale Research, 1962– . Series.

Contemporary Authors "includes nontechnical writers in all genres: fiction, nonfiction, poetry, drama, etc.—whose books are issued by commercial, risk publishers or by university presses. Authors of books published only by known vanity or author-subsidized firms are ordinarily not included. Since native language and nationality have no bearing on inclusion in *CA*, authors who write in languages other than English are included in *CA* if their works have been published in the United States or translated into English. . . . The editors make every effort to secure information directly from the authors through questionnaires and personal correspondence. If writers of special interest to *CA* users are deceased or fail to reply to requests for information, material is gathered from other reliable sources" (Preface, v. 126). Entries include writers deceased since 1900.

Entries are in alphabetical order and include personal data (birthdate, death date where applicable, family, education, address), information on the subject's career and association memberships, as well as sidelights, avocational interests, a bibliography of writings, biographical-critical sources, and, for some, transcripts of interviews. Obituary notices appear in the alphabetical order of the biographical entries.

1. As examples of the diversity of the writers' careers, look up, in volume 126, Henry Moore, internationally famous sculptor; Walter A. McDougall, professor of history with a Pulitzer Prize in history; Warren Beaty (professional spelling, Warren Beatty), actor-director-screenwriter; and two authors whom you might not consider "contemporary," James Joyce and Franz Kafka. The articles on Joyce and Kafka are long and include bibliographies of their writings by genre, correspondence, and critical works.

2. "The key to locating an individual author's listing is the *CA* cumulative index bound into the back of alternate original volumes (and available separately as an offprint). Since the *CA* cumulative index provides access to *all* entries in the *CA* series, the latest cumulative index should always be consulted to find the specific volume containing an author's original or most recently revised sketch" (p. xii). The index also includes references to entries in the related Gale literary series.

The *Contemporary Author* series in current publication includes, in addition to the original volumes, the *CA New Revision, CA Autobiography,* and *CA Bibliographical Series.* To try to lessen confusion in the citations of these and two other series no longer being issued, an explanation of the numbering system of the volumes and a volume update chart are provided in the preface (as of volume 126).

CT
100
C8

CURRENT BIOGRAPHY, 1940–
N.Y., H. W. Wilson, 1940– . il.

Current Biography provides "biographical articles about living leaders in all fields of human accomplishment the world over" (Preface). The series is published in eleven monthly issues, followed by the cumulated yearbook, which includes biographies updated from previous volumes. "Immediately after they are published in the eleven monthly issues, articles are submitted to biographees to give them an opportunity to suggest corrections in time for publication of the *Current Biography Yearbook*" (Preface).

In the front of the yearbooks, there are explanations of the listing of names and pseudonyms and sources, and keys to abbreviations and pronunciation.

At the beginning of each article, there is a portrait of the biographee and a listing of the date of birth, occupation, and address. At the end of the articles, additional biographical sources are listed in two alphabets—one for newspapers and periodicals and one for books.

At the back of the yearbooks you will find photo credits, obituaries (with citations of yearbooks in which biographical articles appeared, and the sources of the obituaries), biographical references, periodicals and newspapers consulted, a classification by profession, and a cumulated index to the preceding volumes for a ten-year period.

The examples given below are from the 1987 *Yearbook*.

1. Look through several *Current Biography Yearbooks* to see the variety of careers and fields of interest represented. The 1987 volume includes Vigdis Finnbogadottir, president of Iceland (note the interesting explanation of Icelandic names); Michael Douglas, actor; Mathilde Krim, research scientist and philanthropist; and Daniel Inouye, U.S. senator. The article on Senator Inouye (the pronunciation of his name is indicated) is an update of one that appeared in the 1960 *Yearbook*.

2. Biographies of those who became prominent as a result of involvement in public issues, national or international, may provide as much or more information on the incident as on the individual, as found in the coverage of Robert Gale, M.D., and Rear Admiral John M. Poindexter.

3. As used in the title of this series, "current" has an elastic application in terms of when the individuals achieved public recognition. The biographees for each yearbook are selected from those who recently came to popular or influential standing, as, for 1987, Sarah, Duchess of York, and Jackie Joyner-Kersee; but it also includes those of long-distinguished prominence, as the ballerina Alexandra Danilova, and those who have had previous articles updated.

4. Excerpts of interviews and quotations from critical analyses supplement the biographical information on authors. Read the articles on Frances FitzGerald, Stanley Elkin, and Frederick Forsyth as examples of the use of multiple, brief commentaries.

5. The classification by profession, which appears at the end of each yearbook, can be helpful in assisting students with assignments on career opportunities or selecting a biography of a person associated with a subject being studied.

Current Biography: Cumulative Index, 1940–1985
Edited by Mary E. Kiffer
N.Y., H. W. Wilson, 1986.

E
176
D562

DICTIONARY OF AMERICAN BIOGRAPHY
**Published under the auspices of the
American Council of Learned Societies**
N.Y., Scribner's, 1928–37. 20v. and index.
Supplements 1– ; 1944– . Reprint: N.Y.,
Scribner's, 1946. 11v.

The *DAB* is a scholarly American biographical dictionary that resembles, by design, the distinguished British *Dictionary of National Biography* (q.v.). The articles are lengthy, written and signed by experts, with bibliographies. Only deceased persons are included. For the most part the entries are Americans, but foreign persons are included if their contribution to the growth and character of the United States was significant.

The original twenty-volume set was reissued, without change of content, in an eleven-volume edition, called the subscription edition. (Supplements 1 and 2 comprise volume 11.)

1. In volume 1, there is a section entitled "Brief Account of the Enterprise," which gives you an understanding of the plan and scope of the project.

2. As examples of the length and content of articles for presidents, look up Thomas Jefferson and Abraham Lincoln.

    For the diversity of occupations and contributions of the biographees, see the entries for Thomas Hart Benton (1782–1858), Walt Whitman, Collis Potter Huntington, and Samuel Gompers.

3. The index volume represents a monumental task of detailed analysis, and it was compiled without computers! The introduction to the index on pages v–vi is helpful.

    The volume citations in the subscription edition index refer to the original twenty-volume set. However, in the introduction to the index of the subscription edition, there is a table that enables the user to transpose the volume numbers of the original set to the volume and part of the later edition. The pagination was not affected in the reprinting. As an example, if you look in the index, Subjects of Biographies, for the poet, Sidney Lanier, you will find:
    Lanier, Sidney Feb. 3, 1842–Sept. 7, 1881.
    X-601 (Edwin Mims)
    Turn to the table in the introduction (p.v.). You will see in the column labeled "Original Edition," volume X, and to the right

under "Subscription Edition," volume V. part 2. The page number, 601, remains the same. The biography was written by Edwin Mims.

The index is useful in several ways. Turn to the section "Birthplaces—United States," which is followed by "Birthplaces—Foreign Countries." Another section reveals which schools and colleges the biographees attended or with which they were closely associated.

The section on occupations is particularly interesting. Notice how many librarians made their way into the *DAB*. Biographees include colonial and early national leaders, pioneers, desperados, industrialists, and twentieth-century authors, actors, scholars, government representatives, and sports figures.

The final section of the index, "Topics," is most impressive. "Under this heading have been included distinctive topics about which there are definite statements and discussions and not merely the mention of the topic" (p. 475). Look at the listings under *Revolution, American.*

4. As an example of the supplements, examine the *Seventh Supplement* published in 1981 and covering the years 1961 through 1965. It contains biographies of 572 persons, written by more than four hundred authors. Read the biography written for Moses, Anna Mary Robertson ("Grandma"; Sept. 7, 1860–Dec. 13, 1961, folk painter). Note the warmth of the writing style and the quotations from the artist. The locations of her paintings and a bibliography for additional reading are included. There is a biography of President John F. Kennedy. In the long roster you will also find General Douglas MacArthur, Edward R. Murrow, and Lorraine Hansberry. Look up the names of the contributors for each of these.

In Supplement 8 (1988), choose several notable biographees to see what biobibliographical information is given.

The *DAB* provides us with an invaluable, continuously useful reference source.

DA	**DICTIONARY OF NATIONAL BIOGRAPHY**
28	**Founded in 1882 by George Smith**
D47	London, Oxford University Press, since 1917. 22v.
	With 1st supplement.

The *Dictionary of National Biography* is regarded as a definitive, scholarly biographical work. A note in the beginning of volume 1 will help you understand the various editions of this monumental British publication, usually referred to as the *DNB*. Following the initial publication covering "from the earliest times to 1900," supplements have brought the work forward; the *9th Supplement* covers 1971–80 (published in 1986). Each edition has a cumulative index from 1901 in one alphabetical series. Entries do not include living persons.

1. A memoir of George Smith, the founder and proprietor of the *Dictionary of National Biography*, written by Sidney Lee, appears in the beginning of volume 1 following the list of contributors. In less than forty pages the brilliant career of an unusual man is revealed against a background of the English literary, business, and publishing worlds of the nineteenth century. Smith, a "problem child," became a genius in the business world and had the rare ability to combine business with artistic and intellectual achievement.

2. Look on page 425 of volume 1 for Anne Boleyn. Where is Anne of Cleves? You should use the index of this volume.

3. The biographees in the *DNB* represent a remarkable range of personalities and accomplishments. Many articles are written in a rather personal style, exhibiting admiration or critical frankness about their subjects but retaining the long-standing reputation of the *DNB* for authoritative coverage. Bibliographies at the end of the entries provide sources for additional research.
   Turn to the *8th Supplement* (1961–70):
   (a) There is a fascinating article about Sir Winston Churchill (pages 193–215!); following which is a listing of the paintings and sculptures of Churchill with their locations, and an annotated bibliography of biographical works. (b) As an example of one of the interesting features of the *DNB*, see the detailed physical description given in the article about Nancy Astor. (c) To get the full flavor of a contributor's style and outspoken comment, read the article about Sir Richard Llewellyn Roger Atcherley.

4. Look through the *9th Supplement* to learn what notable personalities are included.

———. *Supplements.* London, Oxford University Press, 1917– .

AS
911
N9N59

NOBEL PRIZE WINNERS:
An H. W. Wilson Biographical Dictionary
Edited by Tyler Wasson
N.Y., H. W. Wilson, 1987. xxxiv, 1,165p. il.

"Nobel Prize Winners is a biographical reference work containing profiles of all 566 men, women, and institutions that have received the Nobel Prize between 1901 and 1986 . . . placing special emphasis on the body of work for which they were awarded the Nobel Prize" (Preface, p. xxi).

At the beginning of the book, there is a list of Nobel Prize winners in alphabetical order and a list of winners by prize category and year, followed by the names of contributors to this work. Two introductory essays provide a biography of the founder of the awards, Alfred Nobel, and "explain the origin of the Nobel Prize, the criteria governing the selection of laureates, and the significance of the awards" (Preface, p. xxi).

The biographical profiles are arranged alphabetically. Each has a photograph and a bibliography of works by and/or about the subject. In the instances in which a prize was awarded jointly to two or three persons, a separate biography is given for each.

As a cross-reference device, the names of laureates mentioned in biographies of others appear in small capital letters. As an example, see the profile on Enrico Fermi.

1. The bibliographies include only works available in English, but these are supplemented by other titles cited in the profiles. After reading the explanation of the bibliographies in the preface (p. xxii), read the profiles on Selma Lagerlöf, Fritz Haber, and Odysseus Elytis.

2. In the history of the Nobel Prize, some awards have created minor to major challenging questions. Explanations of the controversies are given, countered with statements made at the awards presentations and subsequent observations by those familiar with the life and work of the laureates, as found in the coverage of Albert Schweitzer, Pearl Buck, Aleksandr Solzhenitsyn, Mother Teresa, and Martin Luther King, Jr. Do you think the issues included are relevant to the awards?

3. Albert Bruce Sabin and Jonas Edward Salk, who developed different but successful vaccines for the prevention of poliomyelitis, are not

among the listed winners of the Nobel Prize for Medicine. Do they qualify according to the criteria for awarding the prize?

4. For examples of awards given to other than individuals, refer to the articles on the International Labour Organisation and the International Committee of the Red Cross.

5. In looking at the list of winners of the prize for literature, you will probably find the names of many authors unknown to you. It is a good reminder that all of the world's great literature is not written in nor translated into English.

CT
3260
N57

NOTABLE AMERICAN WOMEN:
A Biographical Dictionary
Cambridge, Mass., Belknap Press of
Harvard University Press, 1971. 3v.

This scholarly, well-received biographical dictionary is additional evidence of the greatly increasing recognition of women. Prepared under the auspices of Radcliffe College, it was modeled after the *Dictionary of American Biography* (q.v.). Of the nearly 15,000 people included in the original *DAB*, only approximately 700 were women. *Notable American Women* corrects that imbalance.

The biographies begin with the year 1607, extend to the twentieth century, and are limited to women who died no later than the end of 1950. Among the biographees "only five women were born after 1900: Jean Harlow, Alice Kober, Carole Lombard, Margaret Mitchell, and Grace Moore" (Preface, p. ix). Women who were not U.S. citizens, but lived in the United States and achieved public recognition here, are included. The editors state they exercised no moral judgment; a few of the notorious are among the women included. (Belle Starr is among the biographees, but was not located in the classified list at the end of volume 3.) "Only one group of women, the wives of the presidents of the United States, were admitted to *Notable Women* on their husbands' credentials. For the others the criterion was distinction in their own right of more than local significance" (Preface, p. xi).

Most of the articles are signed and are followed by excellent bibliographies. As you read the preface you will find a very interesting discussion of the unique problems found in compiling authoritative biographies of women. The introduction provides a historical survey of the part played by women in American history.

1. Do you have a favorite woman in American history, or a favorite performer or leader among the women of the past? See if she is included. Remember the closing date for inclusion of biographees.

2. Turn to the article on Louisa May Alcott. Following the detailed biographical data, there are several columns giving the background of her books. Some of the comments by this famous children's author on her own work might shock you, if you have not previously read a comprehensive biography. The bibliography at the end gives the locations of the manuscript collections, a published full bibliography, annotations on biographies, and other works.

3. The entry for Lucy Ellen Sewall, an early woman physician, gives a very good example of the scholarly and time-consuming research required to obtain information from multiple, "pieced together" sources. This will become clear when you read the bibliography for this article.

4. Among the more contemporary women included is the acclaimed singer Grace Moore. The biography describes her courageous persistence in obtaining her goal in opera.

5. At the end of volume 3, there is a section entitled "Classified List of Selected Biographies" with headings that represent many of the activities and experiences of American women, including abolitionists, actresses, authors (by literary period), Indian captives, political figures, and women's club leaders.

————: *The Modern Period: A Biographical Dictionary.* Edited by Barbara Sicherman [and others]. Cambridge, Mass., Belknap Press of Harvard University Press, 1980. 773p.

The supplement includes 442 biographies of women who died between January 1, 1951, and December 31, 1975.

Read the preface to learn what considerations were used for selecting the subjects and what efforts were made to expand representation. Look through the volume for an overview of who is included. This is an important work with a unique scope and high quality of coverage.

The supplement, like the original three-volume set, includes signed articles, bibliographies, and a classified list of biographies.

CT
213
V36

WEBSTER'S AMERICAN BIOGRAPHIES
Charles Van Doren, Editor;
Robert McHenry, Associate Editor
Springfield, Mass., Merriam-Webster, 1984. xii, 1,233p.

Webster's American Biographies presents 3,082 biographical subjects for whom a criterion of selection was what the editors describe as a "significant contribution" to American life and history. Other criteria include what the editors term "look-up-ableness" (i.e., names of interest to contemporary readers) and "catholicity" of coverage by geographical regions and groups. The subjects are not limited to those born in the United States, but they must have spent some time here.

Several aids for use have been provided. Much effort is evident in the provision of cross-references from nicknames, pseudonyms, and stage names to either the best-known name or the true name. There are two indexes: the first is geographical, by country of birth (and for the U.S., by state), and the second is an index of careers and professions. Some subjects are listed under more than one field, such as Albert Bruce Sabin, who is found under both *immunologists* and *medical figures.*

Dates of birth (and death, if applicable) are cited immediately after the subject's name. If you fail to note the absence of an end date, you could assume from the wording of some of the articles that the person is no longer living.

1. In the introduction the editor states that the first criterion for inclusion in this volume was "significant contribution" or impact in a particular field. If this were so, one wonders at the omission in the field of music of such notables as Enrico Caruso, Vladimir Horowitz, Beverly Sills, and Harry Belafonte. Among the authors, the omission of such names as Jessamyn West, Flannery O'Connor, Laura Ingalls Wilder, and women poets who have achieved national recognition and awards is puzzling. Among the chosen is Hedda Hopper.

   There is unevenness in the coverage of U.S. presidents' wives. Some are identified in the articles on their husbands. Although there are separate articles on Abigal Adams and Eleanor Roosevelt, at least two notable wives are not included: the wife of Woodrow Wilson (Edith Bolling Gault, who is described in contemporary history as a woman of extraordinary influence) and the wife of John F. Kennedy (Jacqueline Bouvier).

   Entries include figures in sports, as Stanley Frank Musial and

William Lee Shoemaker; in the arts, as Charles and Louis Tiffany, Alfred Lunt and Lynn Fontanne, and Eugene Ormandy; in entertainment, as Charles Ringling, Mae West, and John Wayne.

2. Many of the biographies reflect the editors' success in their effort to provide more than vital statistics and to describe the lives "in the context of surrounding events" (Introduction). For examples of this, read the articles on Robert E. Lee, Joseph Welch, Ralph Nader, Bill Mauldin, and Sam Rayburn.

3. Look up Oscar Hammerstein, II, the famous lyricist. In addition to the brief biography, the musicals and most popular songs for which he wrote the lyrics are listed. This complete coverage is given to other composers and lyricists.

4. In assisting a student with the geographical index for an assignment to report on a famous person born in a certain country or state, you should be aware that a biographee might be listed under one place where fame was achieved, and a second location for place of birth, as for the actress Greta Garbo who is listed under *California* and *Sweden*.

CT
103
W4

WEBSTER'S NEW BIOGRAPHICAL DICTIONARY
Springfield, Mass., Merriam-Webster, 1988.
xviii, 1,130p.

This Merriam-Webster publication is a standard ready-reference source. "The present work, while based firmly on its predecessor, is wholly revised and reedited to meet new demands. . . . One major change in the coverage of the book should be noted here: Living persons, whose biographies are virtually impossible to keep up-to-date in a book of this nature, are not included. . . . *Webster's New Biographical Dictionary* takes as its job to present in a single volume biographical information on important, celebrated, or notorious figures from the last five thousand years, beginning with Menes, king of Egypt c. 3100 B.C., and continuing through some 30,000 more" (Preface).

In the front of the book you will find detailed explanatory notes. It is essential to read these for proficient use of this biographical dictionary. The explanatory notes are followed by guides to pronunciation, abbreviations, and pronunciation symbols. At the end of the book there are pronouncing lists of name elements, titles, and pre-names.

1. An outstanding feature of this work is the provision of full names with cross-references for variant spellings for pseudonyms, nick-names, rulers' names, professional names, and religious names— any names known to identify the biographee. Look up the entries for Ernest Pyle, Edith Stein, Frank O'Connor and Connie Mack.

2. The listings of names of saints, popes, rulers, members of royal families, and "major" families may seem complex. If so, refer again to the explanatory notes in the front of the volume, then locate Henry the Navigator, 1394–1460; Saint John of the Cross; and read the first entry for Bach.

    As stated in the preface, the biographies include notorious fig-ures, such as Jean Laffite, Jesse James, Alphonse Capone, and Belle Starr.

3. Titles of works of authors, lyricists, composers and artists are cited, as can be noted in the entries for Robert Schumann, Richard Rodgers, Zurbaran, and Henrik Ibsen. Are the titles of Ibsen trans-lated into English? Translated titles are not given for all foreign-language authors, as Federico Garcia Lorca, Molière, and Andre Malraux.

4. How are the names of Evelyn Waugh and Ngaio Marsh pro-nounced? Remember the section on pronouncing lists of name elements, titles, and prenames at the end of the book, and the keys to pronunciation on pages xii–xv and xviii.

DA
28
W6

**WHO'S WHO An Annual
Biographical Dictionary**
London, A. &. C. Black; New York,
St. Martin's Press, 1849– . Annual.

This internationally known British publication was the springboard for the countless "who's who" titles to follow. It includes brief biog-raphies of outstanding persons in all fields and throughout the world. "The attitude of the present editorial board remains that of the editor of the 1897 edition, who stated in his preface that the book seeks to recognize people 'whether their prominence is inherited, or depending upon office, or the result of ability which singles them out from their fellows in occupations open to every educated man or woman. . . . It cannot be stated too emphatically that inclusion in *Who's Who* has never at any time been a matter for payment or of obligation to purchase the volume" (Preface).

The entries are in alphabetical order.

1. In the front section, note the extraordinary length of the list of abbreviations. An obituary section follows that cites the name, title if applicable, and date of death.

   Preceding the alphabetized entries in the text, the titles, names, vital statistics, and addresses of the English royal family are given.

2. In the 1987 edition, turn to the entry for Yousuf Karsch, the internationally known portrait photographer. His professional credits, exhibits, awards, publications, and recreations are included.

   As further examples of what information is provided, look up the answers to the following:
   a. In what year did Mother Teresa win the Nobel Prize for Peace?
   b. Has Alec Guinness appeared in theater productions in addition to motion pictures?
   c. Does Itzhak Perlman live in the United States?
   d. What public office does Andrew Young hold?

   Can you find entries for nationally or internationally famous persons in sports?

E
176
W642

WHO'S WHO IN AMERICA

Wilmette, Ill., Marquis Who's Who, A Macmillan
Directory Division, 1899–   . Biennial.

"First published in 1899, *Who's Who in America* has become the standard of contemporary biography throughout the nation. The 'Big Red Book' is known for its readily available store of life and career data on noteworthy individuals . . . in Canada and Mexico as well as the United States" (Preface). The concise biographical data is presented in a uniform format, providing a frequently used ready-reference source.

1. Read the preface and standards of admission. There is a sample entry, a table of abbreviations, and an explanation of alphabetical practices.

2. The following are examples of questions that can be answered through *Who's Who in America, 1986–1987*:
   a. What publications awards has Arthur Schlesinger, Jr., received? On what library boards does he serve?
   b. What is the birthdate of Kareem Abdul-Jabbar?
   c. What orchestra is currently under the direction of Seiji Ozawa?
   d. What is the address of the novelist John Irving?

3. Special sections at the end of volume 2 include a retiree index, a necrology, and a list of the names of persons included in the *Marquis Who's Who Regional and Topical Directories*, which supplement the national *Who's Who*.

WILSON AUTHORS SERIES
N.Y., H. W. Wilson, 1942– .
Twentieth Century Authors, 1942.
Edited by Stanley Jasspon Kunitz
and Howard Haycraft
————. *First Supplement*, 1955.
Edited by Stanley Jasspon Kunitz and Vineta Colby.
World Authors, 1950–1970, 1975.
Edited by John Wakeman.
World Authors, 1970–1975, 1980.
Edited by John Wakeman.
World Authors, 1975–1980, 1985.
Edited by Vineta Colby.

The editorial policy of the *World Authors Series* is to provide "authentic biographical information on the writers of this century, of all nations, whose books are familiar to readers of English" (Preface, *World Authors, 1975–1980*). The initial volume, *Twentieth Century Authors*, was followed by the *First Supplement*, which added biographees and updated information on those who appeared in the first volume. The updating of articles was discontinued in the subsequent companion volumes.

The citations and examples given here are from *World Authors, 1975–1980* (1985), unless otherwise noted. In this edition the international representation has been expanded, and for those authors the "sole criterion for selection has been the existence of a portion of their work in English translation" (Preface). The works of those who write in languages other than English are cited in the original language, with the titles of English translation in parentheses or, when there are none, the literal English-language equivalents. In addition to works by the author, the bibliographies include selected biographical and critical sources.

The selection of authors is not limited to those who achieved prominence in the years cited in the edition titles, nor is it limited by subject field—the criteria for the latter being that the work of the author is of wide interest or influence.

The autobiographies create a diversity of style, coverage, and length. The biographical sketches are not signed, but a list of contributors is provided. The critical analysis is intended to give a balanced overall view of the author's work.

Additional features include the pronunciations of names, when considered necessary, shown at the bottom of the first column of the article and based on the key to pronunciation found in the front of the volume, and photographs of many of the biographees. *See* references for pseudonyms and forms of names used are provided in the alphabetical order of the text.

1. For a perspective of the time span of this series, look up in *Twentieth Century Authors* the poets Wilfrid Owen and "H. D." (note the alphabetical placement of this pseudonym). There is a brief updating of information on "H. D." in the *First Supplement.*

2. Autobiographies vary, from the note by Robert Francis to the rather brief account by Dee Brown, who combined a career as a librarian with very successful publications, to the lengthy, self-revealing recollections of Oriana Fallaci, Marilyn French, and Thomas M. Disch.

3. The range of professional fields of the selected authors is represented in the articles on Audre Lorde, Ada Louise Huxtable, and Lewis Thomas.

4. The differences in the detail and scope of the critical analyses of the authors' works can be found in the articles on Carl Sagan and Chingiz Aitmatov. The article on Aitmatov also provides a good example of the citations of original and translated titles given in the text and in the bibliography. The pronunciation of his name is indicated at the bottom of the first column.

5. Look through the companion volumes of 1950–70/1970–75, and read the sketches on several authors whose writings are unknown to you. It is an absorbing way to add to the associations of authors

with titles and experts with subject fields so essential in reference service.

Index to the Wilson Authors Series, revised ed. N.Y., H. W. Wilson, 1986.

CHILDREN'S AND YOUNG ADULT SOURCES

Z
5301
B77

INDEX TO COLLECTIVE BIOGRAPHIES FOR YOUNG READERS, 4th ed.
By Karen Breen
N.Y., R. R. Bowker, 1988. xxxiii, 494p.

This index "grew out of the constant need that faces all librarians working with students to provide short biographical material about historic and contemporary figures of note" (Preface). The books indexed were selected for elementary and junior high school reading levels, but some of the titles may be of interest to high school students. "The *Index* aims to be inclusive rather than selective; the inclusion of a title does not imply that it is a recommended work. . . .

"The book has two main sections. The first, Alphabetical Listing of Biographees, contains pertinent data about birth, death, nationality, and field of activity, followed by symbols indicating in which titles the person's biography appears. The second section, Subject Listing of Biographees, lists these persons under fields of activity and nationalities" (Preface).

1. Read the section "How to Use This Book." This is followed by the key to indexed books, which gives the symbols and citations for over one thousand collective biographies, including out-of-print titles.

2. In the alphabetical listing of biographees, look up (a) Abigail Adams, for whom no nationality is listed, which denotes that she was an American. What do the daggers after two of the symbols indicate? (b) James Bridger, who is identified as a pioneer, scout. Turn to the section "Subject Listing of Biographees," where you will find him listed under *pioneers and frontier people;* but at the heading *scouts* there is a *see* reference to *pioneers and frontier people.*

3. Look through the section "Subject Listing of Biographees" to discover the careers and nationalities included, the many *see also* references, and the divisions by country for certain subjects, as physicians and surgeons, immigrants to United States, and under *musicians* by instrument.

4. The section "Indexed Books by Title" gives the bibliographic data for the collective biographies (with the abbreviation "o.p." if the work is out-of-print) and the names of the biographees included in each book.

5. The final section is the key to publishers, with addresses.

PN
1009
A1

**JUNIOR AUTHORS AND
ILLUSTRATORS SERIES**
N.Y., H. W. Wilson, 1935–   .
The Junior Book of Authors, 1935, revised ed., 1951.
Edited by Stanley Jasspon Kunitz and Howard
Haycraft.
More Junior Authors, 1963. Edited by Muriel Fuller.
Third Book of Junior Authors, 1972. Edited by Doris
de Montreville and Donna Hill.
Fourth Book of Junior Authors and Illustrators, 1978.
Edited by Doris de Montreville and Elizabeth D.
Crawford.
Fifth Book of Junior Authors and Illustrators, 1983.
Edited by Sally Holmes Holtze.

The first volume in the *Junior Authors and Illustrators Series* was published in 1935. The citations and examples given here are from the *Fifth Book.*

"Abounding with anecdote and personal observation, the volumes . . . provide young readers with a direct way of learning more about their favorite authors and books" (Preface, p. v). With successive editions, features have been added to increase the usefulness of the series: bibliographies of selected works by and about the authors, increased recognition of illustrators (including the addition of "illustrators" to the titles with the *Fourth Book*), and a cumulative index to the entire series in each volume.

In selecting those to be included in the *Fifth Book of Junior Authors and Illustrators,* "several aspects of a candidate's work were considered: awards and honors won; the recommendations of reviews and criticism and the appearance of titles on recommended lists; and popularity" (Preface, p. v–vi). Final selection was made by an advisory committee of children's and young adult literature specialists.

"Sketches are arranged in alphabetical order by that version of an author's or illustrator's name appearing most often on title pages" (Preface, p. vi). Cross-references for pseudonyms are provided in the index. Many of the sketches include photographs, reproductions of signatures if authorized, and phonetic pronunciations of names when considered necessary. Bibliographies do not include adult books, books not published in the United States, or, for the most part, strictly critical works.

1. As examples of the differences in styles found in the autobiographical and biographical sketches, read those by Robert Lipsyte and Jack Kent and about Jamake Highwater and Kin Platt.

   Some of the autobiographical articles are quite lengthy in descriptions of personal philosophy and experiences. If you use this work as a ready-reference source, you will probably have to leaf past those to the supplementary biographical sections which provide more of the "vital statistics."

2. The work and influence of librarians in children's literature can be appreciated in the autobiographical contributions of Nancy Bond, Arlene Mosel, and T. Ernesto Bethancourt.

3. Interesting approaches to the illustration of children's books are described in the sketches on Jill Krementz, David Macaulay, and Janet Ahlberg.

4. Turn to the cumulative index at the end of the volume. Some of your favorite childhood authors or illustrators may be included in the earlier volumes with autobiographical sketches. In reading about them you might recall, with nostalgic pleasure, how much and why you enjoyed their work, and how much they added to your early understanding of the worth of books.

PN
451
S6

SOMETHING ABOUT THE AUTHOR:
Facts and Pictures about Authors
and Illustrators of Books for Young People
Edited by Anne Commire
Detroit, Gale Research, 1971–   . Series.

This series is the children's authors' counterpart of *Contemporary Authors* (q.v.). "The *SATA* series includes not only well-known authors and illustrators whose books are most widely read, but also those less prominent people whose works are just coming to be recognized" (Introduction). The authors are primarily from English-speaking countries, but include those from other countries whose works are available in English translation; they are not limited to the contemporary. Each volume (since volume 25) includes revised, updated articles for selected authors and (since volume 20) obituaries providing biographies and bibliographies.

The contents lists in alphabetical order the biographees found in the volume. There are cumulative indexes for authors and illustrators (including citations for entries in other Gale Research biographical series) and a character index (as of volume 50) that "lists selected characters from books and other media created by the authors and illustrators who appear in *Something About the Author (SATA)* and in its companion series, *Yesterday's Authors of Books for Children*" (v. 54, p. 183).

The entries for the authors and illustrators include personal data, information on careers, writings (listed by works for children and, when applicable, for adults), work in progress, hobbies, and additional sources of information. Special features of *SATA* are the reproductions of illustrations from the works and adaptations and photographs of the biographees.

1. In volume 54 (1989), the authors range in style and periods from Rachel Isadore, to P. L. Travers, to Robert Southey.

   See the long article on P. L. Travers, with the illustrations from her books, from the movie *Mary Poppins*, and a record album cover. A full page is given to an illustration by Leo and Diane Dillon. Are they listed in the illustrations index?

   As an example of a comparable article on an illustrator, see the entry for Chris Van Allsburg in volume 53.

PN
1009
A1T9

TWENTIETH-CENTURY CHILDREN'S WRITERS, 2d ed.
Edited by D. L. Kirkpatrick,
with a preface by Naomi Lewis
N.Y., St. Martin's Press, 1983. xvi, 1,024p.

"*Twentieth-Century Children's Writers* includes English-language authors of fiction, poetry, and drama for children and young people. . . . The main part of the book covers writers most of whose work for children was published after 1900; the appendix is of some important representative writers of the later 19th century" (Editor's Note).

The work is arranged in alphabetical order by author. For each writer there is a very brief biography, a bibliography of works for children, and a separate listing of publications for adults (if any), followed by a signed critical essay. For some living authors, their own comments on their writings for children are included. Bibliographies include works illustrated by the authors but written by others, as in the entry for Maurice Sendak.

The preface is an interesting review of children's literature of the period covered in the book. There is also, in the front section, a list of advisers and contributors and one of writers included in the main section and appendix.

1. Because many contributors wrote the critical essays, you will become aware of varied styles, attitudes, and evaluations. Read the entries for Robert Cormier, Peter Dickinson, and Laura Ingalls Wilder.

    In the appendix section on selected writers of the later nineteenth century, read the entry for Howard Pyle as an example of the evaluations of these authors. There is no explanation of the contents of this section except in the editor's note at the beginning of the book. The appendix includes a list of foreign-language writers, preceded by an article by Anthea Bell on translated children's books.

2. In the title index the last name of the author, given in parenthesis, is used instead of a page number for location of an entry.

    At the end of the book there are notes on advisers and contributors.

BIOGRAPHICAL SOURCES

Additional Titles

Abridged Biography and Genealogy Master Index. Edited by Barbara McNeil. Detroit, Gale Research, 1988. 3v.

American Reformers. Edited by Alden Whitman. N.Y., H. W. Wilson, 1985.

Concise biographies, written by historians and subject specialists, of a wide range of U.S. reformers from seventeenth century to the present. Select bibliographies.

Biographical Directory of the United States Congress, 1774–1988, bicentennial ed. Washington, D.C., U.S. Government Printing Office, 1989.

Children's Authors and Illustrators: An Index to Biographical Dictionaries, 4th ed. Edited by Joyce Nakamura. Detroit, Gale Research, 1987.

Comprehensive; aims to include all known writers and illustrators of children's books whose work is accessible in English.

Columbia Dictionary of Modern European Literature, 2d ed. Edited by Jean-Albert Bede and William B. Edgerton. N.Y., Columbia University Press, 1980.

Dictionary of Literary Biography, v. 1– . Detroit, Gale Research, 1978– . In progress.

Series, individual volumes available.

Facts about the Presidents, 4th ed. By Joseph Nathan Kane. N.Y., H. W. Wilson, 1981.

————, *Supplement,* 1985.

Notable Americans: What They Did, from 1620 to the Present: Chronological and Organizational Listings of Leaders, 4th ed. Edited by Linda S. Hubbard. Detroit, Gale Research, 1988.

Pseudonyms and Nicknames Dictionary, 3d ed. Edited by Jennifer Mossman. Detroit, Gale Research, 1987. 2v. *New Pseudonyms and Nicknames* [Supplement to *Pseudonyms and Nicknames Dictionary*] Detroit, Gale Research, 1988.

Who Was When? A Dictionary of Contemporaries, 3d ed. By Miriam A. DeFord and Joan S. Jackson. N.Y., H. W. Wilson, 1976. Chronological list of birth and death dates of influential figures from 500 B.C. to 1974, categorized in ten fields of activity.

Who's Who in American Politics. N.Y., R. R. Bowker, 1967– . Biennial.

On federal, state, local and "other policy makers."

Who's Who of American Women, 1958/59– . Chicago, Marquis Who's Who, 1958– . Biennial.

8.

ATLASES, GAZETTEERS AND GUIDEBOOKS

> . . . in traveling
> a man must carry knowledge with him,
> if he would bring home knowledge.
> James Boswell, *The Life of Samuel Johnson*

The possibilities of seeing the world now seem limitless. Even the universe has become accessible. The discoveries and routes, the locations and descriptions are given to us in maps, gazetteers and travel books. Whether you travel vicariously, are seeking adventure for the first time, or are a sophisticated traveler, you look for and appreciate clarity, readability and accuracy in maps and geographical information.

Meeting the needs of travelers, however, is only one function of geographical source books in a library. Readers, students, advertisers, people changing job location or residence are constantly seeking information that can be obtained from an atlas, gazetteer, or guidebook.

Ecology has become a focus of widespread public thought and discussion. Our dependence on natural resources and the use or abuse of our environment are of critical concern. People turn to libraries for information on water sources, conservation, forests, oceans, crops, climate, and energy sources.

In this chapter, we examine a few atlases, gazetteers, and additional titles as examples of the many more that are available.

ATLASES

Because atlases come in so many different formats, the unskilled user frequently finds it difficult to locate needed information. The librarian, however, should become skilled, not only in their use but also in their selection. Comprehensive atlases are expensive, and the librarian's responsibility is to make a prudent selection. Remember that a number of respected professional periodicals provide reviews of current reference publications. Sources include *Booklist, Choice, Library Journal,* and *Wilson Library Bulletin.*

Although the criteria for selecting reference books in general are applicable to the selection of atlases, the scrutiny of certain characteristics peculiar to atlases may make the difference between a wise selection and an unfortunate one. Essential considerations include:

1. *Authority.* In evaluating an atlas, it is important to determine the authority, not only of the publisher and editor, but also, and more importantly, of the mapmaker. The cartographer's identity is usually printed on the map; if not, it should be indicated in the introductory pages or with the list of contributors.

2. *Accuracy.* You can check the accuracy of an atlas in various ways. Look up a place that is very familiar to you and see if it is clearly indicated where you know it is supposed to be. Compare specific areas shown on the map with the same areas in another similar atlas, the accuracy of which has already been confirmed. The textual and statistical sections can be verified by spot checking or comparison with other authoritative sources, such as an encyclopedia or almanac.

   The names and spellings of place names should consistently follow national or international standards.

3. *Recency.* The necessity of having an up-to-date atlas is readily apparent in our rapidly changing world.

   The timeliness of an atlas needs to be checked. The copyright date of the maps may be quite different from the copyright date of the atlas. Sometimes, in fact, the atlas publisher has nothing to do with cartography, but simply buys a set of maps published by another firm. The maps purchased may be recent or outdated. The copyright date of the maps should be verified before purchasing the atlas.

   Just as continuous revision of encyclopedias is becoming the accepted standard practice, the continuous revision of atlases is also needed.

   To supplement the atlases in a library and to be assured of an up-to-date map collection, libraries might acquire individual maps from such sources as the National Geographic Society and the Superintendent of Documents.

4. *Arrangement.* The arrangement of atlases varies according to the plan or ingenuity of the publisher, but the user should be able to find needed information easily. Essentially, the grouping of the maps should follow a logical sequence. Usually the maps make up the main section of the volume and are followed by a detailed index of place names.

5. *Scope.* Customarily, an atlas published in the United States devotes more space to the United States and less to other parts of the world than foreign atlases, which reverse the priority. There are exceptions, however, an encouraging trend. As with other reference books, the concern is with the purported scope and whether the work succeeds in its stated objectives. Some publishers attempt to enhance the sale of their product by including extras, such as tables, charts, and miscellaneous lists that may or may not be useful, or gazetteer information that may or may not be recent. Such things should be examined realistically to determine their usefulness.

6. *Appearance of maps.* This is one of the crucial features to be considered in the selection of an atlas. Maps should be clear, readable, understandable, and attractive. If a map combines political, physical, and thematic features on a small scale, the result is usually clutter and confusion. The scales should be clearly indicated so that the user can determine the exact distances between places. Another feature to look for is the use of inset maps showing a section of a country, state, or city on a larger scale.

To see the comparative sizes of continents, one or more world maps should be included. A good atlas shows various views of the world by means of different projections, depicting and explaining the distortions that occur when a curved area is placed on a flat surface. On a thematic map, the legend of colors and symbols should be readily located. The print should be clear and readable, and the colors contrasting and pleasing. The guides along the margins should be easily seen, as should the parallels and meridians.

7. *Index.* The index, which usually follows the sequence of maps, should refer the user to the map page or number and to a specific location on the map. Although some atlases indicate the location by longitude and latitude figures, many use letter and number symbols for each grid (the squares made by the parallels and meridians). Some atlases include gazetteer information in the general

index, which may be of additional value. It is important to have cross-references, especially if foreign place names are used, such as Moskova for Moscow. The explanation of the index and its symbols should be explicit.

8. *General format.* An atlas that cannot be opened flat on a desk or table is difficult to use. The binding should be sturdy; the paper should be of high quality to provide good color reproduction and opacity, with page margins ample and the print sharp and legible.

9. *Special features.* As indicated above, some atlases are unnecessarily "padded." On the other hand, those that include special thematic, relief, and/or aerial survey maps, and maps of outer space are definitely enhanced.

10. *Price and the collection.* The library budget must, of course, be considered when an atlas is to be purchased. Within the above criteria, the selection should meet the needs of the particular library for in-library reference use and for circulation.

GAZETTEERS

Gazetteers—geographical dictionaries—complement and supplement atlases. A good gazetteer provides more information about specific places than the gazetteer information frequently found in atlases. Identification of places, with correct spelling, pronunciation, location, and population are the basic items included. Some gazetteers go far beyond these basics and include facts about the history, economy, physical features, and places of interest. They are excellent sources for ready reference. Up-to-dateness is important. The librarian quoting figures from a gazetteer must be cognizant of, and advise the reader of, the copyright date and source of the facts or figures requested.

TRAVEL GUIDES

Travel guides are a versatile part of a library's collection. Besides providing information for travelers—the inexperienced, the sophisticated, and the armchair dreamer—guidebooks have multiple uses in reference service. They provide answers to questions on historical and architectural landmarks, museums, libraries, holidays, customs, food, climate, and culture, and on locations of nations, regions, states, cities, and villages. Sometimes they provide historical background.

There are travel books to suit every need. Among the series that have become particularly popular are the *Baedeker* handbooks (Stuttgart, Baedeker; Englewood Cliffs, N.J., Prentice-Hall), which became classics in the field several generations ago. They provided for each locale, historical background and meticulous place descriptions in a style that seemed equivalent to having a personal native guide. Now issued in new editions, the Baedeker series continues to give detailed, fascinating information supplemented with street maps, diagrams of places of interest (from cathedrals to zoological gardens), and photographic illustrations.

As an example of the coverage, the guidebook on Germany includes a rather lengthy entry on Regensburg, in which the reader is advised that "the best view of Regensburg is from the 310-m long Stone Bridge over the Danube (12th c.), a masterpiece of medieval engineering. Downstream is the Nibelungen Bridge. A short distance from the Stone Bridge is the hub of the city's life, the Domplatz, in which is the Cathedral (13–16th c.; R.C.), the finest Gothic building in Bavaria. . . . The Cathedral has a famous boy's choir, the "Domspatzen" ('cathedral sparrows')."

Other popular series of travel books include *Fodor's Guides* (N.Y., Fodor's Travel Publications) and *Fielding's Guides* (N.Y., Fielding Publications/William Morrow).

In *Fodor's* guide to France, note the sections on French food, the French way of life, and the map of Paris. You might enjoy the descriptions and historical backgrounds of Chartres and Normandy. Compare this guide to *Fielding's* or other travel books of your choice.

The guides to the states and regions of the United States provide similar coverage. Additionally, the *American Guide* series has been a notable and valuable reference source since its creation in the Great Depression by the Federal Writers Project of the Works Progress Administration. Various publishers have reprinted these or published updated, revised editions. Look carefully at one of these guides to appreciate the detailed information on the states, including their history, communities, and points of special interest.

GOODE'S WORLD ATLAS, 17th ed.
Edward B. Espenshade, Editor;
Joel L. Morrison, Senior Consultant
Chicago, Rand McNally, 1986. 384p. maps.

Goode's World Atlas, first published over sixty years ago, retains the name of the original editor and distinguished cartographer, J. Paul Goode, "to affirm the high standards which all those who have participated in the preparation of the book during these years have sought to retain" (p. vi).

The maps are grouped into sections, beginning with "World Thematic Maps"; the second section is entitled "Major Cities Maps." The main body of the atlas is the regional section, which includes detailed physical-political and ocean floor maps. At the end of the atlas there are geographical tables; a glossary of foreign geographical terms, abbreviations, pronunciations of geographical names and terms; and an index.

1. The introduction describes the contents of the atlas and the map scales and projections, and explains the map terms. Read the interesting short illustrated article, "Remotely Sensed Imagery."

2. Look through the world thematic maps, which present multiple features, including climate, landforms, crops, minerals, languages, and population.

3. To evaluate the use of color, see the vast desert areas in the maps of Australia, and the lakes and rivers of central Africa.
   In the section "Major Cities Maps," study the maps of a U.S. city and a foreign city. Do you think there is enough clear detail in these maps?

4. Locate the town of King of Prussia on a map of Pennsylvania by using the pronouncing index. Do you find the symbols used to indicate locations easy to follow?

GUIDE TO PLACES OF THE WORLD
London, Reader's Digest Association, 1987.
736p. il. maps.

There is no preface or introduction to this work; however, the contents are listed under the main headings of: "*A–Z gazetteer*: All the nations of the world, their major cities, towns and geographical features, described and mapped in nearly 8000 separate entries; *Major natural features*: Their structure, how they were formed and their importance in shaping our environment; *World Records*: The biggest, longest, widest, highest and deepest in both the natural and man-made worlds; *Flags of the world*; and *International organisations."* There is a list of contributors in the front of the book. It is notably a British publication.

This is a fascinating book, for with the usual facts, figures, and maps of a gazetteer, interesting, descriptive details have been added on persons, occurrences, and/or special features that have affected or contribute to the uniqueness of the thousands of places entered.

Entries are in word-for-word alphabetical order. Full use has been made of cross references, which are indicated in small capitals. Map locations are cited at the end of the entries. Read the entry for Katherine Gorge, *Australia*, then find it on the map listed: Map Australia Ea.

1. As an example of the coverage of nations, turn to the article on Mexico. In addition to a map, a history is given with a description of the nation's cultural heritage. There is an inset of "Mexico at a Glance" which provides facts and statistics. As a follow-up, see the article on Mexico City.

   There is a long article on the United States, providing historical background; a description of political, social, and economic conditions; facts "at a glance"; color photos; and a map. There is a brief, separate entry for each state, the capitals and largest cities.

2. The *Guide* includes information on occurrences of major national and international interest. In the article on Kiev (Kiyev, Kyiv), *USSR*, a report is given on the 1986 "world's worst recorded civil nuclear accident" at Chernobyl'. (There is a cross-reference: Chernobyl' *USSR see* Kiev.) The entry for Marseilles, France, describes the origin of the French national anthem, *La Marseillaise.*

3. Special features are (a) explanations and cutaway drawings of geographical/geological phenomena, as "The Changing Pattern of the Coasts," p. 212; "How Water Shapes the Land," p. 548; "How Glaciers Change the Landscape," p. 259; and (b) charts giving figures on the longest, highest, widest, etc., as waterfalls, bridges, skyscrapers, rivers, etc.

4. Terms are defined, as *dust bowl, savannah,* and *mud flat.* If you look up *tidal wave,* you will find an instruction and cross-reference: incorrect name for a *tsunami.*

5. In a work as comprehensive as this, there is no end to our expectations, but entries, of course, must be selected by the editors to meet the purpose of the work within reasonable and budgetary limits. As examples, there are entries in the *Guide* for national parks of the world, as the Kruger, South Africa, and Yosemite, California, but not for Uluru, Australia, though it is mentioned in a related entry. In looking up the Murray River, Australia, if you were intrigued by the name of one of the tributaries listed, the Murrunbidgee, which does not have a separate entry, where else could you look to find out its length and where it meets the Murray River?

6. The color photographs, with the beauty of the scenes and the informative captions, add to the value of the *Guide.*

G   **HAMMOND AMBASSADOR WORLD ATLAS**
1021   Maplewood, N.J., Hammond, 1988. xxxii, 484p. maps.
H265

"As in previous editions, the atlas is organized to make the retrieval of information as simple and quick as possible. The guiding principle in organizing the atlas material has been to present separate subjects on separate maps. . . . The basic reference map of an area is accompanied on adjacent pages by all supplementary information pertaining to that area" (Introduction).

Following the table of contents, the introduction to the maps and indexes offers an important, detailed guide to the use of the atlas.

There is a gazetteer index of the world (page I) which, in a single alphabetical order, lists continents, countries, states, and other major geographical areas, with the area in square miles and square kilometers, population, capital, and map page and index key. This is followed by a glossary of abbreviations and an index to terrain maps.

1. Part 1 is titled "The Physical World: Terrain Maps of Land Forms and Ocean Floors." On the contents page of this section, read the explanation of the creation of the topographic model maps.

    As examples: (a) See the map of the floor of the Pacific Ocean. (b) By using the index to terrain maps, can you locate the Sahara

Desert? (c) The listing for Iceland is Bl/2. Compare that with the map on the facing page, plate 3. The terrain maps are followed by maps of the polar regions.

2. Part 2 contains the general political maps, beginning with the continent of Europe. On the facing pages, there are maps depicting the population distribution of Europe, the vegetation and climate, with color keys.

   On the same or adjacent pages of the political map for each country, there is an index to the map, a color illustration of the national flag, a list of brief facts, and maps showing the terrain and distribution of agriculture, industry, and resources.

   There is a considerable imbalance in the coverage of nations, as can be seen in the grouping of the Near and Middle East and of Africa. Note that the official names of West and East Germany are not cited. Can you easily locate the dividing boundary?

3. Turn to the extensive section on the United States. There is a separate map for each state, supplemented with maps for topography, agriculture, industry and resources; a list of brief facts; an inset showing the location of the state on a map of the fifty states, and, selectively, insets of the largest cities.

4. The index of the world that appears at the end of part 2 "contains a complete alphabetical listing of more than one hundred thousand names shown on all the maps included in this atlas. . . . All index entries for cities and towns in the United States are followed by a five-digit postal ZIP code number applying to the community" (Introduction). Read the introduction to the index for a complete explanation of the entries.

5. Special features found at the back of this atlas include a listing of geographical terms; an illustrated description of map projections; world statistical tables; foreign and U.S. city weather; and tables of airline distances.

G
1019
N28

NATIONAL GEOGRAPHIC ATLAS OF THE WORLD, 5th ed.
Washington, D.C., National Geographic Society, 1981.
385p. maps.

At the beginning of the atlas there are large-scale maps and charts of the universe with a brief, explanatory text. These are followed by special maps of world climate, geologic regions, the theory of plate tectonics, and a fascinating section of maps of the ocean floors.

On page 63 there is a "quick reference" list of major areas and a list of map symbols.

1. Turn to the section on physical maps of the world and individual continents. Look at the map of North America (pp. 42–43). Do you easily find the major features, including the great mountain ranges, rivers, lakes, and deserts? Are the colors helpful? Did you discover that the key to color relief is on the bottom left corner of page 40?

   Note the other special maps preceding the general-reference political maps.

2. One useful feature of this atlas is the data provided on the states. Beginning on page 68 there is a color picture of each state flag and information on the special characteristics, products, resources, area, population, capital, and date of admission to the union. The map number for each is cited. Similar coverage is given for the provinces of Canada and the countries of the world, including the language(s) spoken in foreign countries.

3. The atlas is in metric, but conversion tables are included. Note the use of the metric system in the text on the continental crust on pages 38–39.

4. Use the index to find Makaha Beach Park, Hawaii.

5. The atlas ends with various tables, including geographic comparisons, airline distances in kilometers, metric conversions, figures on temperature and rainfall, major cities and their populations, and a listing of foreign terms and abbreviations used. The comprehensive index completes the atlas.

6. Compare the maps of the Great Lakes of the United States, the islands of the Pacific, and the major cities of the world in this atlas with those in two of the other atlases described or cited in this chapter.

G
1019
B395

THE TIMES ATLAS OF THE WORLD, 7th ed.
Comprehensive ed.
London, Times Books, 1985. 419p. maps.

You will be initially impressed with the imposing size of this atlas, and as you look at the maps you will certainly appreciate the quality of its content. It is stated in the foreword that "the aim has always been to inform, to strive for accuracy, and to be as up-to-date as possible" (p. viii).

Read the foreword, which presents a history of the development of the modern atlas with specific references to the *Times Atlas*. You will learn that "if the definition of a map embraces any depiction of terrain features, whether traced in sand or scratched on stone or bone, then cartography must be reckoned among the most ancient communications, preceding any system of writing by millennia" (p. viii).

1. The number and variety of maps and the amount of information given seem as vast as the format of the atlas. Following the foreword there is a listing of states and territories of the world, with size and population; then follows geographical comparisons; the universe; space flight; earth science; map projections; and lists of symbols and abbreviations. Look through the preliminary section, the index section of the contents pages, and the table of contents.

2. Turn to the plates for *Scotland, North*. The islands off the coast are shown in detail, yet a concept of space is gained in the sweep of the format. Note that the lettering clearly designates place names.

   See the plates, on facing pages, for *Switzerland*; they give an interesting perspective of that nation's geography.

   As examples of the use of color, look at the maps of *Egypt, Libya*, and *Texas*.

3. In the section on U.S. maps, the map of the lower Mississippi provides an excellent overview of the route of the Mississippi River.

4. The cities of *Paris* and *London* and their environs each occupy maps on two facing pages; New York City and Washington, D.C., are shown in insets.

   Use the index-gazetteer to locate Montreal, Canada. Note its location in relation to Ottawa and Toronto, the clear black type used for the names of nearby cities and towns, and the insets for the three cities.

5. Preceding the index-gazetteer there is a glossary, a list of abbreviations, and a transcription of Chinese place names. The index-gazetteer lists more than 200,000 names.

   After using the index, do you agree that there is a marvelous simplicity in finding the location of a place on a map with the symbols provided in this atlas?

Continue with your own comparison of the *Times Atlas of the World* with the *Britannica Atlas* (Chicago, Encyclopaedia Britannica, 1988). Remember the elements to be considered in evaluating an atlas. How do you compare the arrangements, type, clarity, use of color, and the advantages of large formats? Are the cartographers and contributors identified? Is a date cited for the maps or the entire contents?

Do you agree with the summary evaluation given in *General Reference Books for Adults* (q.v.) that "without question, the *Britannica Atlas* is among the most comprehensive and authoritative large-format world atlases on the market today, rivaling even *The Times Atlas of the World*" (p. 169)?

G
103.5
W42

WEBSTER'S NEW GEOGRAPHICAL DICTIONARY
Springfield, Mass., Merriam-Webster, 1984.
xxix, 1,376p. maps.

The objective of this standard ready-reference geographical dictionary, as stated in the preface, "is to provide briefly essential information on spelling, pronunciation, and, depending on the nature of the entry, location, population, size (*e.g.*, area, height, length), economy, and history." Entries "include the world's independent states, dependencies, major administrative subdivisions, largest cities, and significant natural physical features. In addition, a large number of entries of historical interest have been included" (p. vi).

Read the explanatory notes to learn the general and alphabetical arrangement, the kinds of information given in the entries, and the use of cross-references. It is important to understand the alphabetical arrangement of the entries, which is clearly explained. These notes are followed by listings of abbreviations and symbols, pronunciation symbols, geographical terms (in various languages with English equivalents, and in English with foreign-language equivalents), and a description of map projections, with map symbols and a list of maps.

1. As an example of the facts provided for each of the states, turn to the entry for Illinois: the first two numbered parts are for rivers. At number 3, for the state, location, area, population, capital, date, and rank in sequence of admission to the Union are given, with

information on its geography, economy, and history, and a table of facts on the counties. Additionally, you are referred to the table of states that follows the entry for United States of America. There is a full-page map of Illinois with an inset for the Chicago area.

2. For a sampling of the kinds of information that can be found in this geographical dictionary, and for use of its guides and sources, look up the following: (a) Port Hueneme: pronunciation; (b) Belgium Congo, and Auschwitz: *see* references and history; (c) Stavropol Krai: abbreviations S.F.S.R., U.S.S.R.; (d) Marne: description of the river in France, including its major significance in World War I; (e) Memphis, part number 4, ancient city in Lower Egypt: location, history, ruins found, and its Old Testament name with citations from the Bible; (f) Victoria Falls: location in Africa, with date of "discovery."

ATLASES, GAZETTEERS, AND GUIDEBOOKS
Additional Titles

American Place-Names: A Concise and Selective Dictionary for the Continental United States of America. By George R. Stewart. N.Y., Oxford University Press, 1970.

Atlas of American History, 2d revised ed. N.Y., Scribner, 1984.

Cities of the United States: A Compilation of Current Information on Economic, Cultural, Geographic and Social Conditions. Detroit, Gale Research, 1988–89. 4v.
Selected cities in volumes by regions: South; West; Midwest; Northeast. Useful data on history, population, climate, economy, recreation, etc.; parts of text obviously from Chambers of Commerce.

Cities of the World, 3d ed. Edited by Margaret Walsh Young and Susan L. Stetler. Detroit, Gale Research, 1987. 4v.

Historical Atlas of the United States, Centennial ed. Washington, D.C., National Geographic Society, 1988.

Market Guide. N.Y., Editor and Publisher, 1924– . Annual.
Arranged by state and city, with information on population, location, principal industries, retail outlets, newspapers, etc.

New International Atlas. Chicago, Rand McNally, 1986.

New York Times Atlas of the World. N.Y., Times Books, 1988.

Prentice-Hall Universal Atlas. Englewood Cliffs, N.J., Prentice-Hall, 1983.

Rand McNally Commercial Atlas and Marketing Guide. Chicago, Rand McNally, 1876–   . Annual.

The Times Atlas of World History, revised ed. Edited by Geoffrey Barraclough. Maplewood, N.J., Hammond, 1984.

We the People: An Atlas of America's Ethnic Diversity. By James Paul Allen and Eugene James Turner. N.Y., Macmillan, 1988.

From 1980 census data, color-coded maps showing distribution of ethnic groups in U.S. counties. Text and tables include immigration history and settlement patterns. Indexed by place and ethnic population. Bibliography.

Wonderful World of Maps. By James F. Madden. Maplewood, N.J., Hammond, 1986.

For elementary grades.

The World Book Atlas. Chicago, World Book, 1988.

9.

ALTERNATE ROUTES

After learning what the "first choice" of reference books may be to answer a patron's question, you will learn with experience that a chosen source may not in fact provide the answer requested. You will then be required to search in related or similar, "second choice" sources. When even these do not provide an answer, you must recall possible "hidden" sources, books that you have analyzed in the preceding chapters which may have been overlooked because you assume they will not contain the needed information, or that you have used so seldom that their range of content has been forgotten. There will be times when the answer might be available in a work that is currently in use by a patron or is missing. It is then that your knowledge of your collection is really tested. You will inevitably receive questions that will challenge your bibliographic knowledge.

If you are employed in a subject department of a large library or in a special library organized for related fields or a single field, you are responsible for knowing your collection and the standard, important bibliography of the subjects included. Once this is accomplished, the reference work, although certainly not without challenge or interest, does not present the constant diverse challenges of the questions received at the general reference desk of a busy public library. There is seemingly no limit to the range of subjects—simple, complex, superficial, scholarly, sophisticated, routine, singular, or plural. An important factor in your assured effectiveness at a demanding reference desk is that you not underestimate the resources of your collection. You have to keep in mind the coverage of specific reference works and remember that some provide a surprising diversity of information.

Some questions are given here to suggest the use of types of sources which may elude you when you are asked a question on a subject and to show how answers can be found in various sources.

The following approaches and responses to sample questions, most of which are in the "ready reference" category, provide the possibility of using general reference sources, or the circulating collection, in libraries which have small- or medium-sized collections and no online reference service. It is suggested you look up each answer for a review of the sources. You might also locate additional sources.

1. A young student has to find the term for a group, an assembly, of *frogs*. If your encyclopedias, and the available books on frogs or amphibians do not include it, what books feature lists of such terms? A perhaps surprising source is *Bernstein's Reverse Dictionary* (q.v.), found under *Creatures*. A rather unusual list of these terms is also in *Brewer's Dictionary of Phrase and Fable* (q.v.), under *Assemblage*, but it does not include frogs.

2. A patron asks for the telephone number of the Attorney General of Idaho. If your library is not in that state, and it does not have out-of-state telephone directories, you may first relate the question to what you might have on Idaho. If that approach does not provide the answer, redirect your search to what you have in directories. Try the *National Directory of Addresses and Telephone Numbers* (q.v.).

3. An art student asks for a history of the city of Florence, Italy. Before you think of referring the student to the catalog, what are the odds that your collection has a book that is wholly on, or that has enough information about the city to be catalogued under the subject? The second thought might be of a general encyclopedia; however, the student might not be satisfied with only this single source. Consider that the city was especially important in a period of history, as the Renaissance, in art, in cultural or political influence; books on those subjects could provide information of interest. Through your own skimming of the article in an encyclopedia, you might note the name of a famous person associated with the history of the city, about whom you have a biography. Additionally, these books may have bibliographies for further searching, or for the student to consider requesting an inter-library loan. Will you look in an index for articles that might have appeared in general periodicals as different as the *National Geographic* and *Gourmet*? Have you thought of travel books which could give concise facts as a basis for further research?

4. An amateur magician tells you that it is unbelievable that the library has only one book on magic, and that it's not on the shelf. You know that the collection contains several books on the subject, but in checking the catalog you find that there is only a title card. The next step is to determine why there are no listings under

the subject. If you do not have the *Library of Congress Subject Headings* to verify the use of a subject and/or to learn what alternate, related headings are used, remember that important key to your catalog: the tracings on the main entry card. In this instance, by looking up the author card, you find that the subject heading used is *Conjuring.*

5. A patron is writing a letter to the Soviet leader, Mikhail Gorbachev, and requests his address. Do you think it could be easily found? If your collection does not include *Who's Who* (q.v.), look up Gorbachev in *Current Biography* (q.v.). In supplying such information, you must consider the date of the publication and the possible changes in the careers of prominent persons.

6. A teacher is preparing an exhibit for a class project on careers, and is looking for an illustration of the lamp that symbolizes Florence Nightingale. After searching in the adult collection, if you can't find one that is clear and satisfactory, you might discover one in the children's collection. At least one juvenile biography of the legendary nurse has a fine, large illustration of the lamp. Since the pictures in children's books are to help young readers to visualize or identify the subjects described, they can sometimes provide illustrations not found in the adult collection.

7. A routine elementary school assignment is to obtain lists of prefixes, or of homonyms. When multiple, simultaneous requests are made by students for these lists, the provision of sources becomes a problem. It is then well to recall your study of dictionaries, such as Skeat's *Etymological Dictionary of the English Language* (q.v.), which has lists of prefixes, suffixes and homonyms in the appendix.

8. The importance of your approach to obtaining an answer can be shown with a patron's question, "How many square miles constitute the city of Beverly Hills, California?" If you think of the subject as a *place,* you might check an atlas/gazetteer, a geographical dictionary, a descriptive work on California, etc. If you think of it as a *statistic,* look it up with confidence in the *County and City Data Book* (U.S. Bureau of the Census).

Additional sources, other than statistical and geographical, for brief facts about places may be found in works related to literature and history, as you discovered in the *Oxford Companion to American Literature* (q.v.), and the *Dictionary of American History* (q.v.). If you are asked whether "Tin Pan Alley" was really a place, remember *Benet's Reader's Encyclopedia* (q.v.).

When the patron's request requires in-depth or extensive searching, the "reference interview" should ensure an efficient, well-informed approach for a successful search. However, the well-developed interview is not a realistic goal when questions are received on a "ready reference," quick-search basis. One key to effective reference service is what might be called a "flexible focus." Try to avoid "locking in" your approach to a question to the limiting factors presented by a patron, or to the subject emphasis of your own immediate reaction. Take time to consider options of sources that may lead to information that is available in your collection. The ability to consider varied sources, to redirect your search, to associate related subjects, increases with experience and is enhanced by imagination and interest.

10.

COMPUTER SOURCES AND SERVICES

In your study of the preceding chapters you have thought, searched, and worked your way through multiple reference books for a substantial initiation in the use of reference sources. The knowledge developed in studying these works provides an excellent base from which to start building your expertise in searching for information using automated systems. Whether the search is through printed sources or through computerized collections of data (commonly called databases), the essential elements and challenges of reference work remain the same: the association of subjects, of ideas with words, of authors with titles, of specialists with fields, and all of these with particular sources of information.

The terminology of computer-based information services will become increasingly familiar to you as you read the professional literature; attend workshops, training sessions, conferences, and conventions; and gain "hands-on" experience. Computers, or terminals—machines from which data can be transmitted and received—have become commonplace in businesses, homes, schools, and libraries. As you become adept in using the machines, or "hardware," and as you see how computerized sources extend collections by making possible access to a vast universe of data, you will be impressed with the opportunities opened up by such technology.

Computer-assisted reference work is generally referred to as online searching. "Online searching" is the term used to indicate the librarian's direct communication with a computer by entering terms, phrases, or key words that state patrons' questions in a way that can be read by the computer. Answers are then received and analyzed. Frequently, questions or approaches must be revised or corrected to retrieve more accurate or additional information. Bibliographies, indexes, abstracts, directories, dictionaries, and encyclopedias, etc., are now available in computerized formats. As more options become available, it is increasingly important for the reference librarian to understand thoroughly the basic techniques of online searching to determine when it is appropriate to offer choices of format to patrons, as manual sources or online databases or a combination of both. On-

line systems are more regularly used in reference when several concepts are combined in one question; when the subject is not covered,
or not well covered, in available books or print indexes; and when the
information is too current or too obscure to be easily located in
printed sources.

Access to information in computerized format may be more difficult than through traditional print tools, but remember, you might
have considered your earlier study of printed reference sources just as
complex! When you learned to read, you learned to use a certain
language; in using computers to get available information, you must
learn the equivalent of a different language or languages. This is easier
to learn than a foreign language because it has a limited vocabulary
and structure. However, there is no standard database arrangement or
system format, so you must learn various "dialects," or searching
"protocols" and commands. You must become what might be described as multilingual to be able to switch from one database or
system "dialect" to another with ease.

There are sources in print that provide information on what is
available via computerized information retrieval systems and how it
is accessed. Several important directories to what is currently online
are the *Directory of Online Databases* (N.Y., Cuadra/Elsevier); *Data
Base Directory* (White Plains, N.Y., Knowledge Industry); *Encyclopedia of Information Systems and Services, Online Databases Search
Services Directory,* and *Computer-Readable Databases* (Detroit, Gale
Research).

"Getting into" a database is very similar to getting into a printed
index or abstract source: you need the proper terms and headings. To
obtain books on a given subject in a library, you use the Library of
Congress or Sears (H. W. Wilson) subject headings, or adaptations of
these. In the use of print indexes, such as the Wilson indexes you
have already examined, you refer to subject headings or index terms;
in other reference sources you may find a subject index within the
books. This is comparable to online databases, in which subject headings are referred to as thesaurus terms or descriptors. You can also
search by key word(s), just as you can manually in key word indexes
found in a number of reference books, such as the *Encyclopedia of
Associations* (Detroit, Gale Research).

When a question or request for information is received from a
patron for online searching, it must be translated into a search statement by selecting thesaurus terms or key words, or combining key
words and descriptors, with a plan for the search strategy. Learning

particular system commands and database formats is the remaining step between the librarian and the database, and learning these simply requires commitment to and enjoyment of the process of computerized information retrieval, instruction, and study of the professional journals, particularly *Library Hi Tech, Online, Database, RQ,* and *Small Computers in Libraries,* as well as some basic texts (see notes and suggested readings at the end of this chapter).

Many databases are available through vendors, just as reference books are available through dealers. Three major commercial database vendors are: DIALOG Information Services, Mead Data Central (NEXIS/LEXIS), and Maxwell Online, incorporating the former BRS Information Technologies, and Pergamon ORBIT Infoline. There are also suppliers of databases for specialized fields, such as medicine (National Library of Medicine: MEDLINE) and law (Mead Data Central: LEXIS; West Publishing Company: WESTLAW). These would be, of course, selected on the basis of the needs of individual libraries. The vendors provide manuals with directions on how to access the systems and use each of the databases, and offer training seminars and videos designed to show how the systems work.

The crucial factor in providing computer-assisted reference service is the skill with which the librarian handles the reference interview, a skill already recognized as essential to effective searching in traditional printed sources. In beginning a search for requested information, the librarian must try to learn discreetly, but as specifically as possible, what the patron *actually* wants (which is sometimes quite different from what is initially requested), and then consider the question and formulate a plan for searching in appropriate sources. Many librarians use a printed form, frequently called a search strategy worksheet, as a guide when interviewing and developing an approach to the search request to ensure the recording of all such relevant data as the patron's description of the topic, list of key words, terms, synonyms, and related descriptors/concepts; type of material desired (articles, reports, reviews, citations, abstracts, full text); language(s), years of coverage needed; and any additional information the patron might have if alternative approaches are needed.

The reference librarian usually makes the decision as to whether a question should be searched through printed sources or online databases. It is essential to learn what the comparative benefits of online searching are, and to apply this knowledge when considering individual requests. Some patrons may insist on the use of an online database that they have heard of, even though you advise them that the search would be cheaper and easier if done manually. There are no easy rules for deciding when a search should be done one way or the other, just as there are no infallible guides for selecting a source.

Because online searching is faster, the use of the computer might be indicated if speed is a requisite. Certainly, staff time needed per patron is reduced, resulting in the ability to answer a greater number of questions in a given period of time. Most online databases are updated more frequently than printed sources, so current information is more likely to be found. For example, it is possible to search for journal citations regarding a recent advance in medicine, a topic of renewed social interest, or a subject that has had limited but long-standing study, and compile a bibliography in a matter of minutes. Incomplete citations may be easily identified by searching online. Also, different concepts can be combined into one search statement, eliminating the time-consuming and often fruitless task of searching in multiple printed sources. One of the most widely known advantages of online searching is the ability to quickly create a bibliography that is tailor-made for individual patron needs.

The librarian's skill is related to a sound knowledge of what information the individual databases can provide, how many avenues are possible to obtain the needed data, and a combination of patience and imagination in rethinking approaches that have not yielded expected answers.

It is not easy to keep up with the online industry; some databases die each year, while others are merged, rearranged, and developed. In her 1988 overview of the online database field, Martha Williams states that there were 301 publicly available databases in 1975. By 1985 the number was 3,010; the estimated figure for 1988 was almost 4,000.[1] The databases available today are listed in classifications, as:

1. *Bibliographic Records.* This type of database contains full bibliographic citations (author, title, source, section, page, etc.). Many include abstracts of the work. Examples are:
   a. *Magazine Index* (Information Access). Index to articles, reviews, and feature stories from popular, general interest magazines. Subjects are multidisciplinary. Coverage is from 1959 to the present.
   b. *National Newspaper Index* (Information Access). Index to the *Christian Science Monitor,* the *Wall Street Journal,* and the *New York Times* (1972 to date), plus selected indexing of the *Los Angeles Times* and the *Washington Post* (1982 to date).

c. *ERIC* (Educational Resources Information Center). Consists of two main files: "Resources in Education" (1966 to date), and the "Current Index to Journals in Education" (1969 to date).

d. MEDLINE (National Library of Medicine). Indexes articles from over three thousand national and international journals covering biomedical literature from 1966 to the present. Includes abstracts.

e. *Books in Print* (R. R. Bowker). A listing of books currently in print and published in the United States. Updated monthly, the database corresponds to the printed editions of *Books in Print, Subject Guide to Books in Print, Paperbound Books in Print,* and *Forthcoming Books.*

2. *Full text records.* This category provides the bibliographic citation and the complete text of the journal article or other primary source. One example is: NEXIS (Mead Data Central). The Newspapers Library contains the full texts of papers, including *The Christian Science Monitor, Los Angeles Times, New York Times, Washington Post,* and specialized papers, such as the *American Banker* and *Computerworld.* The dates of coverage vary for each publication.

The Magazines Library contains the full texts of magazines including *Adweek, Business Week, Byte, Discover, Forbes, Fortune, Money, Newsweek, Time, The Washington Quarterly,* and more. The dates vary for each publication.

The Wire Services file gives the full text of stories from wire services, including Associated Press, Reuters, TASS (Telegraph Agency of the Soviet Union), United Press International, etc. The coverage dates vary.

3. *Directories.* These contain complete listings of a variety of sources, such as:

a. *D&B Dun's Electronic Yellow Pages* (Dun and Bradstreet). Current coverage (with quarterly updates) of directory information for contractors, construction agencies, banks, manufacturers, insurance, real estate, retail and wholesale businesses, financial services, etc.

b. *Foundation Grants Index* (The Foundation Center). Current listings (with bimonthly updates) of grants given to a variety of organizations by major American philanthropic organizations.

4. *Numeric Data.* This type of database provides information that is statistical, tabular, financial, etc. Examples are:

a. *D&B Donnelley Demographics* (Dun and Bradstreet). Gives demographic data from the 1980 census, and current and five-year projections for the United States as a whole, individual states, counties, cities, or zip code areas. Statistics include population by age, race, sex, household size, income, education, and marital status.

b. *Disclosure* (Disclosure Information Group). An example of a file that combines directory and numeric data. It is current (with weekly updates) and provides comprehensive financial information on over 10,000 companies plus management discussion, trends, and market conditions.

The following are examples of questions that can be quickly and satisfactorily answered by searching online databases, either after a manual search is attempted or as the method of first choice:

1. A patron requests your assistance in finding a story in the *New York Times* that described an appearance of Mrs. Corazon Aquino, president of the Philippines, before the U.S. Congress on about September 18, 1986. After her address, someone told Aquino that she had "hit a home run." The patron wants to know who said it. If the *New York Times* is searched (via NEXIS) by entering the key words "Congress," "Aquino," and "home run," and by modifying the query by date—"and date is 9/1986"—the answer will be found in an article dated September 19, 1986: Senator Robert Dole told Aquino that she had "hit a home run."

2. A researcher is looking for articles on Nicaragua that have been published in the *National Geographic* (Washington, D.C., National Geographic Society) in the past ten years. He considers the job of looking through the multiple printed indexes time consuming and tedious. The reference copy of the printed edition of the *National Geographic Index, 1888–1988* is missing. If you search the *Magazine Index* by entering "Nicaragua" and specifying the publication, JN = National Geographic, citations may be easily retrieved.

3. A sales manager needs the latest estimated population for Columbus, Ohio, and can find only the 1980 census figures. By searching in *D&B Donnelley Demographics*, the requested information, plus a five-year projection, will be provided in a matter of minutes.

These questions are neither complex nor specialized, and so do not require sophisticated searches, but they illustrate how a collection can be expanded beyond the traditional reference tools to quickly and efficiently meet the various information needs of patrons.

There are two issues regarding online searching that remain controversial. The first is whether online searching should be free to patrons, as manual searching is, or whether a fee for using an expensive service should be charged. Those who believe that either the total or partial cost should be met by the users say that, without retrieving all or some of the costs of online searching from the patron, libraries cannot afford to offer such special services. Computerized information retrieval is a demanding service that requires individualized attention, time, and professional expertise.

The fee-or-free controversy grows weaker, however, as online service vendors and database producers take advantage of new technological developments in an effort to stay alive and profitable while responding to the problems of cost. New systems have been designed for novices—patrons or librarians—to make searching easier and more cost-effective. The user follows on-screen instructions and chooses options. These systems save money because accessing and searching is faster and easier. Examples are *BRS After Dark, DIALOG Knowledge Index,* and H. W. Wilson Company's *WILSEARCH.*

During the past four years, databases offered in CD-ROM (Compact Disc-Read Only Memory) and laser disc formats have caused much excitement because they have been presented as a way of bringing the benefits of online searching into libraries without the high costs. Among the attractive features are unlimited searching in large databases without online searching charges, unrestricted patron searching because cost is fixed and predictable, reduced time required for research, and collection enhancement by providing inexpensive access to current information. Examples of basic sources available on CD-ROM are the general and specialized periodical indexes of WILSONDISC (H. W. Wilson), *Books in Print with Book Reviews PLUS* (R. R. Bowker), *Magazine Index on InfoTrac* (Information Access), and *Gale GlobalSearch: ASSOCIATIONS* (Gale Research).

Nancy K. Herther's report, "CD-ROM Year Four: What Have We Learned?" provides a concise summary of the advantages, disadvantages and effects of CD-ROM technology.[2]

The second issue, closely related to the problem of cost, is whether or not users should do their own searching, as they do in printed sources. No matter how "friendly" end-user products are supposed to be, they are not so totally friendly that all patrons can successfully retrieve relevant data without some instruction from the librarian. "Help" buttons, "menus" (program options), and on-screen or written instructions are usually insufficient for obtaining complete, well-searched information.

There are no quick solutions to these problems. They will continue to challenge our professional concepts and traditions, but the solutions should lead eventually to unified standards.

Day to day experience in using a computer greatly reinforces instruction in online searching. It is not wise to short-cut your knowledge. While it may not be necessary to understand all facets of "Boolean logic," such terms as *interface, gateways, hypertext, protocols,* etc., will become a part of your vocabulary. If your library provides an online searching service, you should be able to explain to a patron the terms that describe the systems and methods in use. The books and articles written about computers and library uses of computers now seem limitless. Several titles are cited at the end of this chapter.

Your continuing study of online searching should make apparent the uses and benefits of this remarkable form of reference service. No attempt is made here to offer more than a brief introduction. Descriptions of hardware, terms, and databases have been limited to stay within the scope of *Reference Readiness* as a guide to basic, general reference sources.

Whatever sources we use, whether books, periodicals, microforms, CD-ROM, or online searching, the basis of success for competent, effective, and satisfying reference service will be found in the individual librarian's knowledge, interest, and professional identification.

NOTES

1. Martha E. Williams, "Highlights of the Online Database Field: New Technologies for Online," in *National Online Meeting Proceedings,* 1988 (Medford, N.J., Learned Information, 1988), 1–4.

2. Nancy K. Herther, "CD-ROM Year Four: What Have We Learned?" *Database* 11 (June 1988): 106–108.

SUGGESTED READING

Byerly, Greg. *Online and On-Disc Searching: A Dictionary and Bibliographic Guide*, 2d ed. Englewood, Colo., Libraries Unlimited, 1988.

Glossbrenner, Alfred. *How to Look It Up Online: Get the Information Edge with Your Personal Computer.* N.Y., St. Martin's Press, 1987.

Harter, Stephen P. *Online Information Retrieval.* N.Y., Academic Press, 1986.

Humphrey, Susanne M. and Biagio John Melloni. *Databases: A Primer for Retrieving Information by Computer.* Englewood Cliffs, N.J., Prentice-Hall, 1986.

Katz, William A. *Introduction to Reference Work*, 5th ed. V. 2: Reference Services and Reference Processes. N.Y., McGraw-Hill, 1987.

Maloney, James. "Online Information Services." *ALA World Encyclopedia of Library and Information Services*, 2d ed. Chicago, American Library Association, 1986.

Newlin, Barbara. *Answer Online: Your Guide to Informational Databases.* Berkeley, Calif., Osborne/McGraw-Hill, 1985.

Palmer, Roger C. *Online Reference and Information Retrieval*, 2d ed. Littleton, Colo., Libraries Unlimited, 1987.

Vigil, Peter J. *Online Retrieval: Analysis and Strategy.* N.Y., John Wiley, 1988.

PERIODICALS

Database: The Magazine of Database Reference and Review. Weston, Conn., Database/Online, 1978– . Quarterly.

Library Hi Tech. Ann Arbor, Pierian Press, 1983– . Quarterly.

Online: The Magazine of Online Information Systems. Weston, Conn., Online, 1977– . Quarterly.

RQ. Chicago, American Library Association, 1960– . Quarterly.

Small Computers in Libraries. Westport, Conn., Meckler, 1981– . 11/yr.

A Reminder: many of the periodicals cited in chapter 6 contain articles and reviews of books on online reference work.

11.

SEARCH QUESTIONS

These questions are not complex, nor are they "trick" questions. They are offered to reinforce your recollection of the contents and possible uses of the books described. Answers to all these questions can be found in the works analyzed and/or cited in chapters 1 through 8. Answers to some questions might be found in sources of more than one chapter, as almanacs/atlases, handbooks/biographical dictionaries. With the exception of questions for chapter 2, if you use a general encyclopedia for any answer, cite an additional source other than a second general encyclopedia.

Chapter 1

1. What is the etymology of *catamaran*? Do you know to what *Tamil* refers?
2. Is the salutation *hi* defined as a form of *hello*?
3. What source provides definitions and discussion of the use of *polysyllabic humour* and *pedantic humour*? Do you see two built-in clues in the question?
4. How is the Latin phrase *in camera* used in legal terminology?
5. What is the word for a *bell tower*, particularly a tower that is not part of another building?
6. Who coined the word *Muppet*? What words were combined to form the term?

Chapter 2

7. Where can you find a list, by country and size of collection, of national libraries of the world?
8. Is there a single source that provides a comprehensive history of folk music by country with selected scores?
9. Was *Miranda vs. Arizona* a U.S. Supreme Court case?

10. For a question relating to the life of Anne Frank, where was the concentration camp called Bergen-Belsen located?

11. With different lyrics written for the same music, which came first, the American "My Country 'Tis of Thee," or the British anthem, "God Save the Queen"?

12. Can you find information for a patron on electric power systems engineering?

13. Where did the Italian people who came to the United States in the late 1890s and the early 1900s establish communities?

Chapter 3

14. What are the responsibilities of the National Transportation Safety Board? Who appoints the members of the board?

15. What is the salary of the governor of Massachusetts?

16. Can you find travel information about vaccination requirements and health hazards in foreign countries?

17. Does the state of Arizona observe daylight saving time?

18. Where are the regional offices of the Nuclear Regulatory Commission located?

19. Is there a single source that provides listings of literary agents and awards for writers?

20. What time is it in Cheyenne, Wyoming, when it is 12:00 noon in New York City?

21. In the first five years of the 1980s, how many immigrants from Vietnam came to the United States? In what metropolitan areas do they reside?

22. What is the current strength and number of personnel in the navy and air force of China?

Chapter 4

23. Is it true that Maxwell Anderson wrote the lyrics for the "September Song"?

24. Was the internationally recognized Argentinian writer, Jorges Luis Borges, a librarian?

25. Find a brief critical summary of Malcolm Lowry's novel *Under the Volcano.*

26. In typing a manuscript on the development of the space program,

should the name of a spacecraft be capitalized, placed in quotation marks, or underscored?

27. Can you help a student find an explanation of what the title "Tell-Tale Heart" refers to in the story by Edgar Allan Poe?

28. What famous American authors have used the "Lower East Side" of New York City for their settings?

29. Where can you find summaries and/or outlines of federal laws on civil rights passed in 1964 and 1968?

30. Would you expect *Brewer's* to have a list of *Giants* from legend and history?

31. What is the name of the football team of the University of Washington, Seattle?

Chapter 5

32. When was the present Chief Justice of the U.S. Supreme Court sworn into office? Who appointed him to the court?

33. What source would you search to locate a copy of "Letter from Birmingham City Jail," by Martin Luther King, Jr?

34. The lines of a hymn begin with "Eternal Father, strong to save . . ." After verifying the title of this well-known work, can you find citations of anthologies that include it?

35. What is the address of the U.S. Embassy in Paris? Of the French Embassy in the United States?

36. Who owns the *Wall Street Journal*? What is its subscription rate?

37. Was the autobiography of the great pianist Arthur Rubinstein, written possibly in the late 1970s, widely reviewed?

38. For a local theater production, which source would provide an annotated list of modern comedies that indicates the size of the casts?

39. Is "inherit the wind" a quotation from the Bible? Who wrote the play using it as the title?

40. What source contains a listing of the current committee assignments in the U.S. Senate?

41. Does the *Bibliographic Index* include separately published bibliographies, or only those published as parts of books?

42. A student has to read a short story identified only by the title, "Miss Thompson." Who is the author? Has it been published in collections? By what other title is the story known?

43. What is the address of the national headquarters of the American

Medical Association? How many members does the association have?

44. Can you recommend a source to a researcher who needs a comprehensive bibliography of books written since 1955 on civil rights issues in the United States? Can you find a second source as a check of current titles? Do both of these have subject cross-references?

45. Which novels written by Jean Auel have prehistoric settings?

46. For a student taking a course in children's literature, locate an annotated bibliography with reviews cited for Beverly Cleary's fantasy stories about Ralph the mouse.

47. Which source would list recent government publications on the issues of exporting agricultural products?

48. Are there picture books that would help a child understand the functions of hospitals or to resolve a problem with sibling rivalry?

49. Is *Shardik*, the novel by Richard Adams, considered an allegory?

50. Does the periodical *VOYA* contain reviews of books written for young adults? Where is it indexed?

51. Where can a reader obtain an annotated bibliography of bilingual Russian dictionaries (English-Russian; Russian-English)?

Chapter 7

52. Can you verify that a photograph by American photographer Margaret Bourke-White was used for the cover of the first issue of *Life* magazine?

53. Locate a biography with a bibliography on Wendell L. Willkie, a U.S. presidential candidate in 1940.

54. N. C. Wyeth illustrated notable editions of children's classics. What famous illustrator did he study with? What are some of the titles that he illustrated?

55. Where can you find biographical information on Wilfred Owen, whose poetry reflected his experiences in World War I?

56. What education and experience prepared Margaret Thatcher for election as prime minister of Great Britain?

57. Is it true that Golda Meir, late prime minister of Israel, was once a school teacher in Milwaukee, Wisconsin?

58. Is William III, King of the Netherlands, credited with abolishing slavery in the Dutch West Indies near the date of the U.S. Emancipation Proclamation?

59. For students requesting information on careers, cite three sources listing famous photographers.
60. What category of the Nobel Prize was won by Mairead Corrigan and Betty Williams?

Chapter 8

61. Where is Ayers Rock? What special significance does it have?
62. How large a part of Australia is the "outback" region? Is it in the central area of the country?
63. What is the average rainfall/precipitation in August in Acapulco, Mexico?
64. Use an index to an atlas to locate the Ingrid Christensen Coast.
65. What are the differences between relief, topographical, and physical maps?
66. In the United States, is there really a Women's Rights National Historical Park?
67. On what river is the city of Montreal, Canada, situated? What is the population of the metropolitan area?
68. By studying a map, determine the location of Labrador in relation to Quebec and Newfoundland. When did it become a part of Canada?
69. Locate a color-coded map showing the average temperatures on the continent of Africa.
70. Switzerland has four official languages. Can you find a map identifying what the principal language is in each region and/or metropolitan area?

Index